Treasury Christmas Recipes

From Your Favorite Brand Name Companies

PUBLICATIONS INTERNATIONAL, LTD.

Louis Weber, C.E.O.
Publications International, Ltd.
7373 North Cicero Avenue
Lincolnwood, Illinois 60646

Permission is never granted for commercial purposes.

Manufactured in USA.
h   g   f   e   d   c   b   a

ISBN 0-88176-713-1

Library of Congress Catalog Card Number: 89-62188

Pictured on the front cover (*clockwise from top left*): Double-
Decker Fudge (*page 71*), Turkey with Apple Citrus Stuffing
(*page 44*), Cream Cheese Cutout Cookies (*page 68*),
Chocolate Pixies (*page 71*), Fruit-Filled Thumbprints
(*page 75*), Holiday Egg Nog (*page 10*), Christmas Tree Cake
(*page 66*).

Pictured on the back cover (*top to bottom*): Classic Christmas
Cake (*page 57*), Turkey Cranberry Croissant (*page 51*), Hot
Broccoli Dip (*page 4*), Cinnamon-Raisin Swirl Loaf (*page 21*),
Cherry Waldorf Gelatin (*page 33*).

This holiday collection of recipes is a compilation of
many of your favorite brand name recipes previously
published in Favorite Recipes™ magazine. Gathered into
this one convenient source are not only those most
requested favorites but also tempting new holiday recipes
from these same brand name companies.

Contents

Appetizers, Soups & Beverages

■ Hot Broccoli Dip

6 to 8 servings

- 1 1½-lb. round sourdough bread loaf
- ½ cup finely chopped celery
- ½ cup chopped red pepper
- ¼ cup finely chopped onion
- 2 tablespoons PARKAY Margarine
- 1 lb. VELVEETA Pasteurized Process Cheese Spread, cubed
- 1 10-oz. pkg. frozen chopped broccoli, thawed, drained
- ¼ teaspoon dried rosemary leaves, crushed

Cut slice from top of bread loaf; remove center leaving 1-inch shell. Cut removed bread into bite-size pieces. Cover shell with top. Place on cookie sheet with bread pieces. Bake at 350°, 15 minutes or until hot. In large skillet, saute celery, peppers and onions in margarine. Reduce heat to low. Add process cheese spread; stir until melted. Stir in remaining ingredients; heat thoroughly, stirring constantly. Spoon into bread loaf. Serve hot with toasted bread pieces and vegetable dippers.

Preparation time: 15 minutes

Baking time: 15 minutes

Microwave: Prepare bread loaf as directed. Combine celery, peppers, onions and margarine in 2-quart microwave-safe bowl. Microwave on High 1 minute. Add remaining ingredients; microwave on High 5 to 6 minutes or until hot, stirring after 3 minutes. Spoon into bread loaf. Serve hot with toasted bread pieces and vegetable dippers.

■ Country Italian Soup

Makes about 8 (1-cup) servings

- 1 tablespoon oil
- ½ pound boneless beef, cut into 1-inch cubes
- 1 can (14½ ounces) whole peeled tomatoes, undrained and chopped
- 1 envelope LIPTON® Onion or Beefy Mushroom Recipe Soup Mix
- 3 cups water
- 1 medium onion, cut into chunks
- 1 large stalk celery, cut into 1-inch pieces
- ½ cup sliced carrot
- 1 cup cut green beans
- 1 can (16 ounces) chick peas or garbanzos, rinsed and drained
- ½ cup sliced zucchini
- ¼ cup uncooked elbow macaroni
- ¼ teaspoon oregano

In large saucepan or stockpot, heat oil and brown beef over medium-high heat. Add tomatoes, then onion recipe soup mix blended with water. Simmer uncovered, stirring occasionally, 30 minutes. Add onion, celery, carrot and green beans. Simmer uncovered, stirring occasionally, 30 minutes. Stir in remaining ingredients and simmer uncovered, stirring occasionally, an additional 15 minutes or until vegetables and macaroni are tender. Serve, if desired, with grated Parmesan cheese.

Hot Broccoli Dip

■ Wisconsin Cheese 'n Beer Soup

Makes about 4 (1-cup) servings

2 tablespoons butter or margarine
2 tablespoons all-purpose flour
1 envelope LIPTON® Golden Onion Recipe
    Soup Mix
3 cups milk
1 teaspoon Worcestershire sauce
1 cup shredded Cheddar cheese (about
    4 ounces)
½ cup beer
1 teaspoon prepared mustard

In medium saucepan, melt butter and cook flour over medium heat, stirring constantly, 3 minutes or until bubbling. Stir in golden onion recipe soup mix thoroughly blended with milk and Worcestershire sauce. Bring just to the boiling point, then simmer, stirring occasionally, 10 minutes. Stir in remaining ingredients and simmer, stirring constantly, 5 minutes or until cheese is melted. Garnish, if desired, with additional cheese, chopped red pepper and parsley.

Wisconsin Cheese 'n Beer Soup

■ Baked Artichoke Squares

Makes 24 appetizers

½ cup plus 3 tablespoons CRISCO® Oil,
    divided
1 cup chopped mushrooms
¼ cup thinly sliced celery
1 clove garlic, minced
1 can (13¾ ounces) artichoke hearts,
    drained, chopped
⅓ cup chopped green onions
½ teaspoon dried marjoram, crushed
¼ teaspoon dried oregano, crushed
¼ teaspoon ground red pepper
1 cup (4 ounces) shredded Cheddar cheese
1 cup (4 ounces) shredded Monterey Jack
    cheese
2 eggs, slightly beaten
1½ cups all-purpose flour
½ teaspoon salt
¼ cup milk

Heat 3 tablespoons of the CRISCO oil in medium skillet over medium-high heat. Cook and stir mushrooms, celery and garlic in hot oil until celery is tender. Remove from heat. Stir in artichoke hearts, onions, marjoram, oregano and ground red pepper. Add cheeses and eggs; mix well. Set aside.

Combine flour and salt in medium bowl. Blend remaining ½ cup CRISCO oil and the milk in small bowl. Add to flour mixture. Stir with fork until mixture forms a ball. Press dough in bottom and 1½ inches up sides of 13×9×2-inch pan. Bake in preheated 350°F oven 10 minutes. Spread artichoke mixture on baked crust. Continue baking about 20 minutes more or until center is set. Cool slightly. Cut into 24 squares. Serve warm.

■ Kahlúa® Hot Spiced Apple Cider

Makes 1 serving

1½ ounces KAHLÚA®
1 cup hot apple cider or apple juice
1 cinnamon stick

Pour KAHLÚA® into hot cider. Stir with cinnamon stick.

Traditional Party Mix

■ Traditional Party Mix

Makes 9 cups

¼ cup (½ stick) margarine
1¼ teaspoons seasoned salt
4½ teaspoons worcestershire sauce
2⅔ cups CORN CHEX® Brand Cereal
2⅔ cups RICE CHEX® Brand Cereal
2⅔ cups WHEAT CHEX® Brand Cereal
 1 cup salted mixed nuts
 1 cup pretzel sticks

Preheat oven to 250°. In open roasting pan melt margarine in oven. Remove. Stir in seasoned salt and worcestershire sauce. Gradually add cereals, nuts and pretzels, stirring until all pieces are evenly coated. Bake 1 hour, stirring every 15 minutes. Spread on absorbent paper to cool. Store in airtight container.

*Microwave Directions:** In a 4-quart bowl or 13×9×2-inch microwave-safe dish melt margarine on HIGH 1 minute. Stir in seasoned salt and worcestershire sauce. Gradually add cereals, nuts and pretzels, stirring until all pieces are evenly coated. Microwave on HIGH 5 to 6 minutes, stirring every 2 minutes. Spread on absorbent paper to cool. Store in airtight container.

Due to differences in microwave ovens, cooking time may need adjustment. These directions were developed using 625 to 700 watt ovens.

Christmas Punch

■ Christmas Punch

Makes 8 to 9 cups

> 5 cups DOLE® Pineapple Juice
> 1 bottle (24 oz.) sparkling apple juice or
>   champagne

ICE MOLD
> 1 can (20 oz.) DOLE® Pineapple Chunks
> 1 orange, sliced, quartered
> 1 pint strawberries or bottled maraschino
>   cherries
>   Mint sprigs

Chill punch ingredients. Combine in punch bowl.
Float ice mold when ready to serve.

Ice mold: Combine undrained pineapple, fruit
and mint in 6-cup mold. Add enough water or
juice to fill. Freeze.

■ Stuffed Mushrooms Italiano

Makes about 24 appetizers

> 1 pound large mushrooms
> ¼ cup WISH-BONE® Italian or Caesar
>   Dressing
> 1 cup fresh bread crumbs
> ¼ cup grated Parmesan cheese
> 1 tablespoon finely chopped parsley

Remove and finely chop mushroom stems.
Combine dressing, bread crumbs, cheese, parsley
and chopped mushroom stems in medium bowl.
Fill each mushroom cap with bread crumb
mixture; arrange in shallow baking dish. Add
water to barely cover bottom of dish. Bake in
preheated 350°F oven 20 minutes.

■ Port Cheddar Cheese Spread

Makes about 3 cups

4 cups (1 pound) shredded sharp Cheddar
   cheese
¼ cup butter or margarine, softened
¼ cup dairy sour cream
2 tablespoons port wine
¼ teaspoon ground mace
⅛ teaspoon ground red pepper
1 cup chopped toasted walnuts
   Assorted vegetables for dippers
   Assorted crackers

Combine cheese, butter, sour cream, wine, mace
and ground red pepper in food processor. Cover
and process until smooth. Mix in walnuts.
Refrigerate, covered, several days to allow flavors
to mellow. Soften slightly at room temperature
before serving. Serve with assorted vegetables and
crackers.

Favorite Recipe from **Walnut Marketing Board**

■ Kahlúa® Parisian Coffee

Makes 1 serving

1 ounce cognac or brandy
½ ounce KAHLÚA®
½ ounce Grand Marnier
   Hot coffee
   Whipped cream
   Orange peel (optional)

Pour cognac, KAHLÚA® and Grand Marnier into
steaming cup of coffee. Top with whipped cream.
Garnish with orange peel.

■ Hot Spiced Wine

Makes about 2½ quarts, about 16 (5-ounce) servings

1 quart water
2 cups sugar
25 whole cloves
3 cinnamon sticks
½ lemon, peeled
1 bottle (1.5 L) CRIBARI® Zinfandel

Combine water, sugar, spices and lemon in
medium saucepan. Boil over medium-high heat
until mixture is syrupy. Reduce heat to low. Add
wine; simmer 5 minutes. Do not let wine boil.

■ Easy Vegetable Squares

Makes 32 appetizer servings

2 8-ounce packages refrigerated crescent
   rolls (16 rolls)
1 8-ounce package cream cheese, softened
1 3-ounce package cream cheese, softened
⅓ cup mayonnaise *or* salad dressing
1 teaspoon dried dillweed
1 teaspoon buttermilk salad dressing mix
   (¼ of a 0.4-ounce package)
3 cups desired toppings (see below)
1 cup shredded Wisconsin Cheddar,
   Mozzarella, *or* Monterey Jack cheese

For crust, unroll crescent rolls and pat into a
15½×10½×2-inch baking pan. Bake according to
package directions. Cool.

Meanwhile, in a small mixing bowl stir together
the cream cheese, mayonnaise, dillweed, and
salad dressing mix. Spread evenly over cooled
crust. Sprinkle with desired toppings, then the
shredded Cheddar, Mozzarella, or Monterey Jack
cheese.

Topping options: finely chopped broccoli,
cauliflower, *or* green pepper; seeded and
chopped tomato; thinly sliced green onion, black
olives, *or* celery; *or* shredded carrots.

Preparation time: 20 minutes

Favorite Recipe from **Wisconsin Milk Marketing Board** © 1989

Easy Vegetable Squares

■ Party Chicken Sandwiches

Makes 3 dozen

1½ cups finely chopped cooked chicken
1 cup MIRACLE WHIP Salad Dressing
1 4-oz. can chopped green chilies, drained
¾ cup (3 ozs.) 100% Natural KRAFT Shredded
   Sharp Cheddar Cheese
¼ cup finely chopped onion
36 party rye or pumpernickel bread slices

Combine chicken, salad dressing, chilies, cheese
and onions; mix lightly. Cover bread with chicken
mixture. Broil 5 minutes or until lightly browned.
Serve hot. Garnish as desired.

Preparation time: 15 minutes

Broiling time: 5 minutes

Variation: Substitute MIRACLE WHIP Light
Reduced Calorie Salad Dressing for Regular Salad
Dressing.

■ Coffee Egg Nog Punch

Makes about 1½ quarts

3 cups BORDEN® or MEADOW GOLD® Milk
1 (14-ounce) can EAGLE® Brand Sweetened
   Condensed Milk (NOT evaporated milk)
4 eggs*
3 to 4 teaspoons instant coffee
⅓ cup bourbon
⅓ cup coffee-flavored liqueur
1 cup (½ pint) BORDEN® or MEADOW GOLD®
   Whipping Cream, whipped
   Dash ground cinnamon
   Dash ground nutmeg

In large mixer bowl, combine milk, sweetened
condensed milk, eggs and coffee; beat on low
speed until coffee dissolves. Stir in bourbon and
liqueur; chill. Before serving, top with whipped
cream, cinnamon and nutmeg. Refrigerate
leftovers.

Holiday Egg Nog: Omit instant coffee and coffee-
flavored liqueur. Increase bourbon to ½ cup; add
1 teaspoon vanilla extract. Proceed as above.

Use only Grade A clean, uncracked eggs.

■ Creamy Broccoli Soup

Five 1-cup servings

¼ cup chopped onion
1 tablespoon PARKAY Margarine
2 cups milk
1 8-oz. pkg. PHILADELPHIA BRAND Cream
   Cheese, cubed
¾ lb. VELVEETA Pasteurized Process Cheese
   Spread, cubed
1 10-oz. pkg. frozen chopped broccoli,
   cooked, drained
¼ teaspoon ground nutmeg
   Dash of pepper

In 2-quart saucepan, saute onions in margarine
until tender. Reduce heat to medium. Add milk
and cream cheese; stir until cream cheese is
melted. Add remaining ingredients; heat
thoroughly, stirring occasionally.

Preparation time: 15 minutes

Cooking time: 15 minutes

Variations: Substitute frozen chopped spinach
for broccoli.

Substitute frozen cauliflower, chopped, for
broccoli.

Substitute frozen asparagus spears, chopped, for
broccoli.

Microwave: Microwave onions and margarine in
2-quart microwave-safe bowl on High 30 seconds
or until onions are tender. Add milk; microwave
on High 4 minutes, stirring after 2 minutes. Stir in
cream cheese; microwave on High 4 to 6 minutes
or until cream cheese is melted, stirring every 2
minutes. Stir in remaining ingredients; microwave
on High 30 seconds or until thoroughly heated.

Party Chicken Sandwiches

■ Shrimp Spread

Makes 2 cups

   1 8-oz. pkg. PHILADELPHIA BRAND Cream
      Cheese, softened
   ½ cup MIRACLE WHIP Salad Dressing
   1 4¼-oz. can tiny cocktail shrimp, drained,
      rinsed
   ⅓ cup finely chopped onion
   ⅛ teaspoon garlic salt

Combine cream cheese and salad dressing, mixing
until well blended. Stir in remaining ingredients.
Cover; chill. Serve with assorted crackers.

Preparation time: 10 minutes plus chilling

Shrimp Spread

■ Mexi-Beef Bites

Makes 36 appetizers

   1 pound ground beef
   1 cup (4 ounces) shredded Cheddar cheese
   1 cup (4 ounces) shredded Monterey Jack
      cheese
   1 can (4 ounces) chopped green chilies,
      drained
   ½ cup bottled green taco or enchilada sauce
   2 large eggs, beaten
      Tortilla chips (optional)

Cook and stir beef in large skillet over medium-
high heat until beef loses pink color. Pour off
drippings. Stir in cheeses, chilies, taco sauce and
eggs. Transfer mixture to 8×8-inch baking pan.
Bake at 350°F 35 to 40 minutes or until knife
inserted in center comes out clean and top is
golden brown. Cool in pan 15 minutes. Cut into
36 squares. Serve with tortilla chips.

Favorite Recipe from **National Live Stock and Meat Board**

■ Hot Holiday Punch

Makes 8 (8-ounce) servings

   1 cup granulated sugar
   ½ cup packed brown sugar
   4 cups apple cider
   1 cinnamon stick
  12 whole cloves
   2 cups Florida Grapefruit Juice
   2 cups Florida Orange Juice
      Orange slices
      Maraschino cherry halves (optional)
      Whole cloves (optional)

Combine sugars and apple cider in large
saucepan. Heat over medium heat, stirring until
sugars dissolve. Add cinnamon stick and cloves.
Bring to a boil over medium heat. Reduce heat to
low; simmer 5 minutes. Add grapefruit and orange
juices. Heat, but do not boil. Strain into heatproof
punch bowl. Garnish with orange slices decorated
with maraschino cherry halves and whole cloves.
Serve in heatproof punch cups.

Vegetable Meat Stew

■ Vegetable Meat Stew

Makes 6 servings

  2 tablespoons all-purpose flour
1½ teaspoons salt
  1 teaspoon AC'CENT® Flavor Enhancer
⅛ teaspoon pepper
  1 pound beef stew meat
  3 tablespoons vegetable oil
¼ cup chopped onion
  3 cups water
  1 clove garlic, minced
  1 bay leaf
  1 teaspoon dried thyme, crushed
  4 small potatoes, pared, cubed
  4 carrots, chopped, or 12 mini-carrots, pared
  1 cup frozen peas, thawed
½ cup PET® Evaporated Milk

Combine flour, salt, AC'CENT Flavor Enhancer and pepper in shallow dish. Dredge meat in flour mixture; reserve excess flour mixture. Brown meat in hot oil in Dutch oven over medium-high heat. Sprinkle any remaining flour mixture over meat. Toss to coat meat. Add onion; cook until onion is limp. Add water, garlic, bay leaf and thyme. Bring to a boil over high heat. Reduce heat to low. Cover and simmer 1 hour. Add potatoes, carrots and additional water if needed. Simmer, covered, 15 minutes. Add peas; simmer, covered, 10 minutes or until vegetables are tender. Stir in evaporated milk; heat through. *Do not boil.* Remove bay leaf before serving.

Apple Spice Egg Nog

■ Apple Spice Egg Nog

Makes about 3½ quarts

3 (32-ounce) cans BORDEN® Egg Nog, chilled
3 cups apple cider, chilled
½ teaspoon ground cinnamon

In large bowl, combine ingredients; mix well.
Chill. Garnish as desired. Refrigerate leftovers.

■ Easy Tomato-Cheese Bisque

Makes 5 servings

1 can (11 oz.) condensed cheddar cheese
soup
2 cups water
1 cup tomato juice
1 tablespoon butter or margarine
1 tablespoon chopped chives (optional)
½ teaspoon salt
½ teaspoon sugar
½ teaspoon dry mustard
½ teaspoon Worcestershire sauce
1 cup MINUTE® Rice
¾ cup milk, light cream or evaporated milk

Mix soup with water and tomato juice in large
saucepan. Add butter, chives and seasonings.
Bring to a full boil. Stir in rice and milk. Reduce
heat; cover and simmer 10 minutes, stirring
occasionally. Garnish with additional chopped
chives or popcorn, if desired.

■ Appetizer Ham Logs

Makes about 24 appetizers

2 cups ground ham
1 egg, beaten
¼ teaspoon pepper
¼ cup seasoned fine dry bread crumbs
½ cup horseradish sauce
1 tablespoon prepared mustard
⅛ teaspoon celery salt
Vegetable oil for frying
Pimiento strips

Combine ham, egg and pepper in medium bowl;
mix well. Shape into 1-inch logs or balls. Roll in
bread crumbs. Refrigerate, covered, 1 hour.

To make mustard sauce, combine horseradish
sauce, mustard and celery salt in small bowl until
well blended. Refrigerate, covered, until serving
time.

Heat 3 inches oil in heavy, large saucepan over
medium-high heat until oil is 365°F; adjust heat to
maintain temperature. Fry ham logs, a few at a
time, 2 to 3 minutes or until golden. Drain on
paper towels. Garnish with pimiento strips. Serve
with mustard sauce.

Favorite Recipe from **National Pork Producers Council**

■ Miniature Teriyaki Pork Kabobs

Makes about 24 appetizers

1 pound boneless pork, cut into
4×1×½-inch strips
1 can (11 ounces) mandarin oranges
1 small green bell pepper, cut into
1×¼×¼-inch strips
¼ cup teriyaki sauce
1 tablespoon honey
1 tablespoon vinegar
⅛ teaspoon garlic powder

Soak 24 (8-inch) bamboo skewers in water 10
minutes. Thread pork strips accordion-style with
mandarin oranges on skewers. Place 1 pepper
strip on end of each skewer. Arrange skewers on
broiler pan.

For sauce, combine teriyaki sauce, honey, vinegar
and garlic powder in small bowl; mix well. Brush
sauce over kabobs. Broil, 6 inches from heat,
about 15 minutes or until pork is done, turning
and basting with sauce occasionally.

Favorite Recipe from **National Pork Producers Council**

■ Rumaki

Makes about 32 appetizers

> 16 slices bacon
> 1 pound chicken livers, cut into quarters
> 1 can (8 ounces) sliced water chestnuts, drained
> ⅓ cup soy sauce
> 2 tablespoons packed brown sugar
> 1 tablespoon Dijon-style mustard

Cut bacon slices in half crosswise. Wrap ½ slice bacon around piece of chicken liver and water chestnut slice. Secure with wooden pick. (Reserve any remaining water chestnut slices for another use.) Arrange on broiler pan. Combine soy sauce, brown sugar and mustard in small bowl. Brush over bacon rolls. Broil, 6 inches from heat, 15 to 20 minutes or until bacon is crisp and chicken livers are done, turning and brushing with soy sauce mixture occasionally.

Favorite Recipe from **National Pork Producers Council**

■ Ham-Wrapped Oysters

Makes 24 appetizers

> 3 tablespoons prepared horseradish
> ½ pound ham, cut into 3×1×¼-inch strips
> 2 dozen fresh oysters, shucked
> 3 tablespoons butter or margarine, melted
> 1 tablespoon lemon juice
> ¼ teaspoon garlic powder

Spread horseradish on 1 side of each ham strip. Place 1 oyster on each ham strip; roll up and secure with wooden pick. Arrange on broiler pan. Combine butter, lemon juice and garlic powder in small cup. Brush each ham roll with some of the lemon-butter. Broil, 5 inches from heat, 10 to 15 minutes or until edges of oysters curl, brushing occasionally with the remaining lemon-butter.

Favorite Recipe from **National Pork Producers Council**

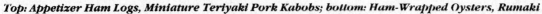

Top: Appetizer Ham Logs, Miniature Teriyaki Pork Kabobs; bottom: Ham-Wrapped Oysters, Rumaki

■ South-of-the-Border Dip

3 cups

- ½ cup chopped onion
- 2 tablespoons PARKAY Margarine
- 1 lb. VELVEETA Mexican Pasteurized Process Cheese Spread with Jalapeño Pepper, cubed
- 1 14½-oz. can tomatoes, chopped, drained

In large skillet, saute onions in margarine; reduce heat to low. Add remaining ingredients; stir until process cheese spread is melted. Serve hot with tortilla chips or vegetable dippers.

Preparation time: 10 minutes

Cooking time: 10 minutes

Microwave: Microwave onions and margarine in 1½-quart microwave-safe bowl on High 1½ minutes or until tender. Add remaining ingredients; mix well. Microwave on High 5 minutes or until thoroughly heated, stirring after 3 minutes. Serve hot with tortilla chips or vegetable dippers.

South-of-the-Border Dip

■ Mulled Cider

Makes about 2 quarts

- 2 quarts apple cider
- ¾ to 1 cup REALEMON® Lemon Juice from Concentrate
- 1 cup firmly packed light brown sugar
- 8 whole cloves
- 2 cinnamon sticks
- ¾ cup rum, optional
  Additional cinnamon sticks, optional

In large saucepan, combine all ingredients except rum and additional cinnamon sticks; bring to a boil. Reduce heat; simmer uncovered 10 minutes. Remove spices; add rum just before serving if desired. Serve hot with cinnamon sticks if desired.

Tip: Can be served cold.

Microwave: In deep 3-quart round baking dish, combine ingredients as above. Heat on 100% power (high) 13 to 14 minutes or until hot. Serve as above.

Sweet 'n' Sour Meatballs

■ Chili Soup Jarlsberg

Makes 6 servings

    1 pound beef round steak, diced
    2 tablespoons vegetable oil
    2 cans (14½ ounces each) ready-to-serve beef
      broth
    1 can (15 ounces) dark red kidney beans
    1 can (14½ ounces) tomatoes, chopped,
      undrained
    1 medium green bell pepper, chopped
    1 medium red bell pepper, chopped
    1 large onion, chopped
    1 large clove garlic, minced
 3¼ teaspoons chili powder, divided
    ¼ teaspoon ground cumin
 1½ cups (6 ounces) shredded Jarlsberg cheese,
      divided
    ¼ cup butter or margarine, softened
    1 small clove garlic, minced
   12 KAVLI Norwegian Crispbreads

Brown beef in hot oil in large, deep saucepan over medium-high heat. Add broth. Bring to a boil over high heat. Reduce heat to low. Cover and simmer 1 hour. Add beans, tomatoes, peppers, onion, large garlic clove, 3 teaspoons of the chili powder and the cumin. Simmer, covered, 30 minutes. Gradually blend in ½ cup of the Jarlsberg cheese. Heat just until cheese melts.

Blend butter, small garlic clove and remaining ¼ teaspoon chili powder in small bowl. Spread on crispbreads; arrange on cookie sheet. Bake in preheated 375°F oven several minutes or until butter is melted. Sprinkle with ½ cup of the Jarlsberg. Bake just until cheese is melted.

Ladle soup into bowls. Garnish with remaining ½ cup Jarlsberg. Serve with crispbreads.

Favorite Recipe from **Norseland Foods, Inc.**

■ Kahlúa® & Coffee

Makes 1 serving

 1½ ounces KAHLÚA®
      Hot coffee
      Whipped cream (optional)

Pour KAHLÚA® into steaming cup of coffee. Top with whipped cream.

■ Sweet 'n' Sour Meatballs

Makes about 5 dozen

 1½ pounds lean ground beef
    1 (8-ounce) can water chestnuts, drained
      and chopped
    2 eggs
    ⅓ cup dry bread crumbs
    1 tablespoon Worcestershire sauce
    4 teaspoons WYLER'S® or STEERO® Beef-
      Flavor Instant Bouillon
    1 cup water
    ½ cup firmly packed light brown sugar
    ½ cup REALEMON® Lemon Juice from
      Concentrate
    ¼ cup catsup
    2 tablespoons cornstarch
    ¼ teaspoon salt
    1 large red or green pepper, cut into squares
      Chopped parsley, optional

In large bowl, combine meat, water chestnuts, eggs, bread crumbs, Worcestershire and bouillon; mix well. Shape into 1¼-inch meatballs. In large skillet, brown meatballs. Remove from pan; pour off fat. In skillet, combine remaining ingredients except pepper and parsley; mix well. Over medium heat, cook and stir until sauce thickens. Reduce heat. Add meatballs; simmer uncovered 10 minutes. Add pepper; heat through. Garnish with parsley if desired. Refrigerate leftovers.

Breads & Coffee Cakes

■ Cream Cheese Swirl Coffee Cake

Makes one 10-inch cake

2 (3-ounce) packages cream cheese, softened
2 tablespoons confectioners' sugar
2 tablespoons REALEMON® Lemon Juice from Concentrate
2 cups unsifted flour
1 teaspoon baking powder
1 teaspoon baking soda
¼ teaspoon salt
1 cup granulated sugar
½ cup margarine or butter, softened
3 eggs
1 teaspoon vanilla extract
1 (8-ounce) container BORDEN® or MEADOW GOLD® Sour Cream
Cinnamon-Nut Topping (recipe follows)

Preheat oven to 350°. In small bowl, beat cheese, confectioners' sugar and ReaLemon® brand until smooth; set aside. Stir together flour, baking powder, baking soda and salt; set aside. In large mixer bowl, beat granulated sugar and margarine until fluffy. Add eggs and vanilla; mix well. Add dry ingredients alternately with sour cream; mix well. Pour half of batter into greased and floured 10-inch tube pan. Spoon cheese mixture on top of batter to within ½ inch of pan edge. Spoon remaining batter over filling, spreading to pan edge. Sprinkle with Cinnamon-Nut Topping. Bake 40 to 45 minutes or until wooden pick inserted near center comes out clean. Cool 10 minutes; remove from pan. Serve warm.

Cinnamon-Nut Topping: Combine ¼ cup finely chopped nuts, 2 tablespoons granulated sugar and ½ teaspoon ground cinnamon.

■ Streusel Lemon Bread

Makes one 9×5-inch loaf

½ cup finely chopped nuts
¼ cup firmly packed light brown sugar
½ teaspoon ground nutmeg
2 cups unsifted flour
1 teaspoon baking powder
½ teaspoon baking soda
1¼ cups granulated sugar
½ cup margarine or butter, softened
3 eggs
½ cup REALEMON® Lemon Juice from Concentrate
½ cup BORDEN® or MEADOW GOLD® Milk

Preheat oven to 350°. In small bowl, combine nuts, brown sugar and nutmeg; set aside. Stir together flour, baking powder and baking soda; set aside. In large mixer bowl, beat granulated sugar and margarine until fluffy. Add eggs, 1 at a time; beat well. Gradually beat in ReaLemon® brand. Add milk alternately with flour mixture; stir well. Spoon half of batter into greased and floured 9×5-inch loaf pan. Sprinkle half of nut mixture over batter; top with remaining batter, spreading to pan edge. Top with remaining nut mixture. Bake 50 to 55 minutes or until wooden pick inserted near center comes out clean. Cool 15 minutes; remove from pan. Cool completely. Store tightly wrapped.

Cream Cheese Swirl Coffee Cake

18

Pineapple Citrus Muffins

■ Pineapple Citrus Muffins

Makes 12 muffins

⅓ cup honey
¼ cup butter or margarine, softened
1 egg
1 can (8 ounces) DOLE® Crushed Pineapple
1 tablespoon grated orange peel
1 cup all-purpose flour
1 cup whole wheat flour
1½ teaspoons baking powder
¼ teaspoon salt
¼ teaspoon ground nutmeg
1 cup DOLE® Chopped Dates
½ cup chopped walnuts, optional

Preheat oven to 375°F. In large mixer bowl, beat together honey and butter 1 minute. Beat in egg, then undrained pineapple and orange peel. In medium bowl, combine remaining ingredients; stir into pineapple mixture until just blended. Spoon batter into 12 greased muffin cups. Bake in preheated oven 25 minutes or until wooden pick inserted in center comes out clean. Cool slightly in pan before turning out onto wire rack. Serve warm.

■ Golden Pumpkin Bread

Makes 1 loaf

1½ cups all-purpose flour
1 cup packed brown sugar
1 cup solid pack pumpkin
½ cup LAND O LAKES® Sweet Cream Butter, softened
2 eggs
1 teaspoon baking powder
1 teaspoon baking soda
½ teaspoon salt
1½ teaspoons ground cinnamon
½ teaspoon ground cloves
½ teaspoon ground ginger

In large bowl, combine all ingredients; beat until well mixed. Pour into greased 9×5×3-inch loaf pan. Bake in preheated 350° oven 45 to 55 minutes or until wooden pick inserted into center comes out clean. Let cool in pan on wire rack 10 minutes. Loosen edges; remove from pan. Cool completely on wire rack.

■ Banana Nut Bread

Makes 1 loaf

2 extra-ripe, large DOLE® Bananas, peeled
⅓ cup butter
⅔ cup sugar
2 eggs
2 cups all-purpose flour
2 teaspoons baking powder
½ teaspoon baking soda
½ cup buttermilk
¾ cup chopped nuts

Puree bananas in blender (1¼ cups). Cream butter with sugar, until light and fluffy. Beat in bananas and eggs. Combine flour, baking powder and baking soda. Add dry ingredients to banana mixture alternately in thirds with buttermilk, blending well after each addition. Stir in nuts. Pour into greased 9×5-inch loaf pan. Bake in 350°F oven 50 to 60 minutes until tests done. Cool in pan on a rack 10 minutes. Turn out onto rack to complete cooling.

■ Cinnamon-Raisin Swirl Loaf

Makes 2 loaves

2 cups SUN-MAID® Raisins
 Water
6¾ to 7¼ cups all-purpose flour
2 packages active dry yeast
2 cups milk
¾ cup granulated sugar
¼ cup butter or margarine
2 teaspoons salt
3 eggs
2 teaspoons ground cinnamon
 Powdered Sugar Icing (recipe follows)

In small bowl, combine raisins with enough hot tap water to cover. Plump 5 minutes; drain well. Set aside. In large bowl, combine 3 cups of the flour and the yeast. In medium saucepan, heat milk, ¼ cup of the granulated sugar, the butter and salt over low heat just until warm (115° to 120°F) and until butter is almost melted, stirring constantly. Add to flour mixture; add eggs. Beat at low speed of electric mixer for ½ minute, scraping sides of bowl constantly. Beat 3 minutes at high speed, scraping bowl occasionally. Stir in plumped raisins. Stir in as much remaining flour as can be mixed in with a spoon. Turn out onto lightly floured board. Knead in enough remaining

flour to make a moderately stiff dough that is smooth and elastic (6 to 8 minutes total). Shape into a ball. Place dough in lightly greased bowl; turn once to grease surface. Cover; let rise in warm place (85°F) until doubled, about 1¼ hours.

Punch dough down; divide in half. Cover; let rest 10 minutes. Roll each half into 15×7-inch rectangle. Brush entire surface lightly with water. Combine remaining ½ cup granulated sugar and cinnamon; sprinkle ½ of the sugar mixture over each rectangle. Roll up, jelly-roll fashion, starting from a 7-inch side; pinch edges and ends to seal. Place, sealed edges down, in 2 greased 9×5×3-inch loaf pans. Cover; let rise in warm place until nearly doubled, 35 to 45 minutes. Bake in preheated 375°F oven 35 to 40 minutes or until bread sounds hollow when tapped, covering bread with foil the last 15 minutes to prevent overbrowning. Remove bread from pans; cool completely on wire racks. Drizzle with Powdered Sugar Icing.

Powdered Sugar Icing: In medium bowl, combine 1 cup sifted powdered sugar, ¼ teaspoon vanilla and enough milk (about 1½ tablespoons) to make of drizzling consistency.

Cinnamon-Raisin Swirl Loaf

Ladder Coffee Cakes

Makes 2 pastries

½ cup butter
½ cup dairy sour cream
1 cup all-purpose flour
1 cup canned cherry pie filling
¼ cup chopped walnuts (optional)
½ cup sifted powdered sugar
2 teaspoons milk

In a large mixer bowl beat butter on high speed of electric mixer for 30 seconds. Add sour cream; beat until fluffy. Add flour and mix well. Cover and chill dough about 1 hour or until firm enough to handle.

Divide the dough in half. Working with half of the dough at a time, roll to a 10×8-inch rectangle. Place rectangle on a greased baking sheet. Spread *half* of the pie filling lengthwise down the center third of the rectangle. If desired, sprinkle *half* of the chopped walnuts over the pie filling. Make cuts 2½ inches deep at 1-inch intervals along both long sides. Fold strips over filling, pinching into narrow points at center. Repeat with remaining dough. Bake in a 350° oven for 30 minutes or until golden. Remove to wire rack. Sprinkle with additional chopped walnuts, if desired. In a small mixing bowl stir together the powdered sugar and milk. Drizzle over baked pastries. Cut into slices to serve.

Preparation time: 1 hour

Favorite Recipe from **Wisconsin Milk Marketing Board** © 1989

Braided Sesame Ring

Makes 1 loaf

7 to 8 cups all-purpose flour
2 packages active dry yeast
¼ cup sugar
1 teaspoon salt
1½ cups hot water (120° to 130°)
½ cup HELLMAN'S® or BEST FOODS® Real
    Mayonnaise
4 eggs
2 tablespoons sesame seeds

In large bowl, combine 2 cups of the flour, the yeast, sugar and salt. Gradually beat in water until smooth. Add 2 more cups flour, the real mayonnaise and 3 of the eggs; beat well. Stir in enough of the remaining flour to make dough easy to handle. Turn out onto lightly floured surface. Knead 10 minutes or until dough is smooth and elastic, adding as much remaining flour as needed to prevent sticking. Shape dough into ball. Place in large, greased bowl; turn dough once to grease surface. Cover with towel; let rise in warm place (85°) until doubled, about 1 hour.

Punch dough down; divide into 3 equal pieces. Cover; let rest 10 minutes. Roll each piece into 24-inch rope. Place side-by-side on large greased baking sheet; loosely braid ropes. Shape braid into circle, pinching ends together to seal. Cover; let rise in warm place until doubled, about 1½ hours. In small bowl, beat remaining egg; brush over surface of dough. Sprinkle with sesame seeds. Bake in preheated 375° oven 40 minutes or until loaf is browned and sounds hollow when tapped. Remove to wire rack to cool.

Onion-Herb Baked Bread

Makes 1 loaf

1 envelope LIPTON® Golden Onion Recipe
    Soup Mix
1 medium clove garlic, finely chopped
1 teaspoon basil leaves
1 teaspoon oregano
⅛ teaspoon pepper
½ cup butter or margarine, softened
1 loaf Italian or French bread (about 16
    inches long), halved lengthwise

Preheat oven to 375°.

In small bowl, thoroughly blend all ingredients except bread; generously spread on bread halves. On baking sheet, arrange bread, cut side up, and bake 15 minutes or until golden. Serve warm.

Note: Store any remaining spread, covered, in refrigerator for future use.

Ladder Coffee Cake

Chocolate Streusel Coffee Cake

■ Chocolate Streusel Coffee Cake

Makes 12 to 16 servings

Chocolate Streusel (recipe follows)
½ cup butter or margarine, softened
1 cup sugar
3 eggs
1 cup dairy sour cream
1 teaspoon vanilla extract
2 cups all-purpose flour
1 teaspoon baking powder
1 teaspoon baking soda
¼ teaspoon salt

Prepare Chocolate Streusel; set aside. Cream butter and sugar in large mixer bowl until light and fluffy. Add eggs; blend well on low speed. Stir in sour cream and vanilla. Combine flour, baking powder, baking soda and salt; add to batter. Blend well.

Sprinkle 1 cup of the Chocolate Streusel into greased and floured 12-cup Bundt® pan. Spread one-third of the batter (about 1⅓ cups) in pan; sprinkle with half the remaining streusel (about 1 cup). Repeat layers, ending with batter on top. Bake at 350° for 50 to 55 minutes or until cake tester comes out clean. Cool 10 minutes; invert onto serving plate. Cool completely.

Chocolate Streusel

¾ cup packed light brown sugar
¼ cup all-purpose flour
¼ cup butter or margarine, softened
¾ cup chopped nuts
¾ cup HERSHEY'S MINI CHIPS Semi-Sweet Chocolate

Combine brown sugar, flour and butter in medium bowl until crumbly. Stir in nuts and MINI CHIPS Chocolate.

■ Golden Apple Boston Brown Bread

Makes 2 loaves

¼ cup butter or margarine, softened
⅓ cup honey
⅓ cup light molasses
1 cup whole wheat flour
1 cup rye flour
1 cup yellow cornmeal
2 teaspoons baking soda
½ teaspoon salt
2 cups buttermilk
2 cups (2 medium) coarsely chopped Golden Delicious apples

In large bowl, cream butter, honey and molasses. In medium bowl, combine flours, cornmeal, baking soda and salt. Add flour mixture to butter mixture alternately with buttermilk, mixing well after each addition. Stir in apples. Pour batter into 2 greased 8½×4½×2½-inch loaf pans. Bake in preheated 350°F oven 1 hour or until wooden pick inserted near center comes out clean. Let cool in pans on wire racks 10 minutes. Loosen edges; remove from pans. Cool slightly on wire racks; serve warm.

Variation: To steam brown bread, divide batter evenly between 2 greased 1-pound coffee cans, filling cans about three fourths full. Cover tops of cans with aluminum foil; tie foil to cans with string. Place rack in large kettle; add boiling water to depth of 1 inch. Place cans on rack; cover kettle. Steam over low heat 3 hours or until wooden pick inserted near center comes out clean. If necessary, add more boiling water to kettle during steaming. Cool as above.

Favorite Recipe from **Washington Apple Commission**

French Breakfast Puffs

■ Oatmeal Dinner Rolls

Makes 3 dozen rolls

> 2 cups old-fashioned oats, uncooked
> 1½ cups boiling water
> ¼ cup LAND O LAKES® Sweet Cream Butter
> 2 packages active dry yeast
> ½ cup warm water (105° to 115°)
> 6¼ to 7¼ cups all-purpose flour
> 1 cup packed brown sugar
> ⅓ cup light molasses
> 2 eggs
> 1½ teaspoons salt

In medium heatproof bowl, combine oats, boiling water and butter; stir until butter is melted. Cool until warm (105° to 115°). In large bowl, combine yeast and water; stir to dissolve yeast. Stir in oat mixture, 2 cups of the flour, the sugar, molasses, eggs and salt; beat until smooth. Stir in enough of the remaining flour to make dough easy to handle. Turn out onto lightly floured surface. Knead 10 minutes or until dough is smooth and elastic, adding as much remaining flour as needed to prevent sticking. Shape dough into ball. Place in large, greased bowl; turn dough once to grease surface. Cover with towel; let rise in warm place (85°) until doubled, about 1½ hours.

Punch dough down; divide in half. With floured hands, shape each half into 18 smooth balls. Place balls in 2 greased 13×9×2-inch pans. Cover; let rise in warm place until doubled, about 1 hour. Bake in preheated 375° oven 20 to 25 minutes or until golden brown. Remove from pans to wire racks. If desired, brush tops of hot rolls with melted butter; serve warm.

Oatmeal Dinner Rolls

■ French Breakfast Puffs

32 puffs

> 1½ cups unsifted all-purpose flour
> ½ cup confectioners sugar
> 1 teaspoon baking powder
> 1 teaspoon salt
> ¾ teaspoon ground nutmeg
> ½ cup milk
> ½ cup water
> ¼ cup CRISCO® Oil
> 1½ teaspoons grated lemon peel
> 3 eggs
> CRISCO® Oil for frying
> Confectioners sugar

Mix flour, ½ cup confectioners sugar, baking powder, salt and nutmeg in small mixing bowl. Set aside. Combine milk, water, CRISCO Oil and lemon peel in medium saucepan. Heat to rolling boil over medium-high heat. Add flour mixture all at once. Beat with wooden spoon until mixture pulls away from sides of pan into a ball. Remove from heat; cool slightly. Add eggs, one at a time, beating after each addition.

Heat 2 to 3 inches CRISCO Oil in deep-fryer or large saucepan to 350°F.

Drop dough by tablespoonfuls into hot CRISCO Oil. Fry 3 or 4 puffs at a time, 4 to 6 minutes, or until golden brown, turning over several times. Drain on paper towels. Sprinkle top of each puff with confectioners sugar.

Almond Citrus Muffins

Makes 1 dozen muffins

½ cup whole natural almonds
1¼ cups all-purpose flour
2 teaspoons baking powder
¼ teaspoon salt
1 cup shreds of wheat bran cereal
¼ cup packed brown sugar
¾ cup milk
¼ cup orange juice
1 teaspoon grated orange peel
1 egg
¼ cup vegetable or almond oil

Spread almonds in single layer on baking sheet. Bake at 350°F, 12 to 15 minutes, stirring occasionally, until lightly toasted. Cool and chop. Increase oven to 400°F. In large bowl, combine flour, baking powder and salt. In medium bowl, combine cereal, sugar, milk, orange juice and peel. Let stand 2 minutes or until cereal is softened. Add egg and oil; beat well. Stir in almonds. Add liquid mixture to flour mixture; stir just until moistened. Batter will be lumpy; do not over mix. Spoon batter evenly into 12 greased 2½-inch muffin cups. Bake in preheated 400°F oven 20 minutes or until lightly browned. Remove to wire rack to cool.

Favorite Recipe from **Almond Board of California**

Peanut Butter and Jam Swirl Coffee Cake

Makes 1 coffee cake

½ cup milk
⅓ cup packed brown sugar
½ teaspoon salt
1 package active dry yeast
¼ cup warm water (105° to 115°)
1½ to 2½ cups all-purpose flour
¼ cup peanut butter
1 egg
⅓ cup raspberry or strawberry jam

In small saucepan over medium heat, scald milk. In medium heatproof bowl, combine sugar and salt. Add hot milk; stir to dissolve sugar. Cool until warm (105° to 115°). Add yeast to water; stir to dissolve yeast. Add 1 cup of the flour and the peanut butter to milk mixture; beat until smooth. Stir in yeast mixture and egg; beat well. Stir in

enough of the remaining flour to make thick batter; beat well. Cover with waxed paper; let rise in warm place (85°) until bubbly and doubled, about 1 hour. Stir down batter. Spread in well-greased 9-inch round pan. With floured fingers, press spiral-shaped indentation in top of batter, starting at center and working toward outside. Fill indentation with jam. Cover; let rise in warm place until doubled, about 45 minutes. Bake in preheated 350° oven 30 to 35 minutes or until golden brown. Remove to wire rack to cool.

Favorite Recipe from **Oklahoma Peanut Commission**

Cranberry Apple Streusel Coffee Cake

Makes 12 servings

CAKE
2 cups Any AUNT JEMIMA Pancake & Waffle Mix (see Note)
½ cup sugar
1 8-oz. carton sour cream
¾ cup milk
1 egg, beaten
¾ cup chopped cranberries
¾ cup peeled, coarsely chopped apple

STREUSEL
½ cup chopped nuts
¼ cup firmly packed brown sugar
½ teaspoon cinnamon
2 tablespoons margarine, melted

GLAZE
¾ cup powdered sugar
1 tablespoon milk
½ teaspoon vanilla

Heat oven to 350°F. Grease 13×9-inch baking pan. Combine pancake mix and sugar. Add sour cream, milk, and egg; mix just until dry ingredients are moistened. Spread into pan; top with cranberries and apple. Combine streusel ingredients; mix until crumbly. Sprinkle over fruit. Bake 30 to 35 minutes or until wooden pick inserted in center comes out clean. Combine glaze ingredients; drizzle over warm cake. Serve warm. (To reheat cooled cake, microwave each serving at high about 20 seconds.)

Note: AUNT JEMIMA Buttermilk Complete, Complete, Original, Whole Wheat or Lite Buttermilk Complete mixes may be used.

Apricot Date Coffee Cake

■ Apricot Date Coffee Cake

Makes 3 coffee cakes

1 cup warm milk (105° to 115°)
2 packages active dry yeast
1 cup butter, softened
½ cup granulated sugar
2 eggs, slightly beaten
1 teaspoon salt
1 teaspoon ground cardamom
5 to 5½ cups all-purpose flour
1 cup prepared apricot filling
½ cup chopped dates
2 cups sifted powdered sugar
3 tablespoons light cream or half-and-half
½ teaspoon vanilla
¼ teaspoon almond extract

In large bowl, combine milk and yeast; stir to dissolve yeast. Stir in butter, granulated sugar, eggs, salt, cardamom and 2 cups of the flour; beat until smooth. Stir in enough of the remaining flour to make dough easy to handle. Turn out onto lightly floured surface. Knead 10 minutes or until dough is smooth and elastic, adding as much remaining flour as needed to prevent sticking. Shape dough into ball. Place in large, buttered bowl; turn dough once to butter surface. Cover with waxed paper; let rise in warm place (85°) until doubled, about 1½ hours. Meanwhile, in small bowl, combine apricot filling and dates; set aside.

Punch dough down; divide into 3 equal pieces. Roll out one third of dough on lightly floured surface into 12×10-inch rectangle. Spoon one third of apricot mixture down center third of dough. Fold all 4 sides over so they meet at center of filling; pinch to seal. Place dough seam side down on buttered baking sheet. With scissors, snip 1-inch wide strips almost to center on both long sides of coffee cake. Turn each strip on its side to expose filling. Repeat with remaining dough and filling. Cover; let rise in warm place until doubled, about 30 minutes. Bake in preheated 375° oven about 18 minutes or until golden brown. Remove to wire racks to cool completely. In small bowl, combine powdered sugar, cream, vanilla and almond extract; mix well. Drizzle over coffee cakes.

Favorite Recipe from **American Dairy Association**

Lemon Pecan Sticky Rolls

Lemon Pecan Sticky Rolls

Makes 16 rolls

½ cup granulated sugar
½ cup firmly packed light brown sugar
¼ cup margarine or butter
¼ cup REALEMON® Lemon Juice from
   Concentrate
½ teaspoon ground cinnamon
½ cup chopped pecans
2 (8-ounce) packages refrigerated crescent
   rolls

Preheat oven to 375°. In small saucepan, combine sugars, margarine, ReaLemon® brand and cinnamon. Bring to a boil; boil 1 minute. Reserving ¼ *cup,* pour remaining lemon mixture into 9-inch round layer cake pan. Sprinkle with nuts. Separate rolls into 8 rectangles; spread with reserved lemon mixture. Roll up jellyroll-fashion, beginning with short side; seal edges. Cut in half. Place rolls, cut-side down, in prepared pan. Bake 30 to 35 minutes or until dark golden brown. Loosen sides. Immediately turn onto serving plate; do not remove pan. Let stand 5 minutes; remove pan. Serve warm.

Savory Bubble Cheese Bread

Makes one 10-inch round loaf

6 to 7 cups flour, divided
2 tablespoons sugar
4 teaspoons instant minced onion
2 teaspoons salt
2 packages active dry yeast
½ teaspoon caraway seeds
1¾ cups milk
½ cup water
3 tablespoons butter or margarine
1 teaspoon TABASCO® pepper sauce
2 cups (8 ounces) shredded sharp Cheddar
   cheese, divided
1 egg, lightly beaten

In large bowl of electric mixer combine 2½ cups flour, sugar, onion, salt, yeast and caraway seeds. In small saucepan combine milk, water and butter. Heat milk mixture until very warm (120°F. to 130°F.); stir in TABASCO sauce.

With mixer at medium speed gradually add milk mixture to dry ingredients; beat 2 minutes. Add 1 cup flour. Beat at high speed 2 minutes. With wooden spoon stir in 1½ cups cheese and enough flour to make a stiff dough. Turn dough out onto lightly floured surface. Knead 8 to 10 minutes or until dough is smooth and elastic, adding as much remaining flour as needed to prevent sticking. Place in large greased bowl and invert dough to bring greased side up. Cover with towel; let rise in warm place (90°F. to 100°F.) 1 hour or until doubled in bulk.

Punch dough down. Divide dough into 16 equal pieces; shape each piece into a ball. Place ½ the balls in well-greased 10-inch tube pan. Sprinkle with remaining ½ cup cheese. Arrange remaining balls on top. Cover with towel; let rise in warm place 45 minutes or until doubled in bulk. Preheat oven to 375°F. Brush dough with egg. Bake 40 to 50 minutes or until golden brown. Remove from pan. Cool completely on wire rack.

■ Cheese Casserole Bread

Makes 1 loaf

  2 cups warm milk (105° to 115°)
  2 packages active dry yeast
  3 tablespoons sugar
  1 tablespoon butter
  ½ teaspoon salt
4½ cups all-purpose flour
  6 ounces Cheddar cheese, cut into
      ½-inch cubes

In large bowl, combine milk and yeast; stir to dissolve yeast. Add sugar, butter and salt; stir until butter is melted. Stir in 3 cups of the flour; beat until smooth. Stir in remaining flour and cheese; mix well. Pour batter into well-buttered 1½-quart round casserole. Cover with waxed paper; let rise in warm place (85°) until doubled, about 1 hour. Remove waxed paper. Bake in preheated 350° oven 50 to 55 minutes or until wooden pick inserted into center comes out clean. Let cool in dish on wire rack 10 minutes. Loosen edge; remove from dish. Cool slightly on wire rack; serve warm with butter.

Favorite Recipe from **American Dairy Association**

■ Apple-Cranberry Muffins

Makes 1 dozen muffins

1¾ cups plus 2 tablespoons all-purpose flour
  ½ cup sugar
1½ teaspoons baking powder
  ½ teaspoon baking soda
  ½ teaspoon salt
  1 egg
  ¾ cup milk
  ¾ cup sweetened applesauce
  ¼ cup butter or margarine, melted
  1 cup fresh cranberries, coarsely chopped
  ½ teaspoon ground cinnamon

In medium bowl, combine 1¾ cups of the flour, ¼ cup of the sugar, the baking powder, baking soda and salt. In small bowl, combine egg, milk, applesauce and butter; mix well. Add egg mixture to flour mixture; stir just until moistened. Batter will be lumpy; do not over mix. In small bowl, toss cranberries with remaining 2 tablespoons flour; fold into batter. Spoon batter evenly into 12 greased 2¾-inch muffin cups. In measuring cup, combine remaining ¼ cup sugar and the cinnamon. Sprinkle over tops of muffins. Bake in preheated 400° oven 20 to 25 minutes or until golden brown. Remove to wire rack to cool.

Favorite Recipe from **Western New York Apple Growers Association, Inc.**

Cheese Casserole Bread

Salads & Side Dishes

■ Swiss Vegetable Medley

Makes 6 servings

1 bag (16 ounces) frozen vegetable
   combination (broccoli, carrots,
   cauliflower), thawed and drained
1 can (10¾ ounces) condensed cream of
   mushroom soup
1 cup (4 ounces) shredded Swiss cheese
⅓ cup sour cream
¼ teaspoon DURKEE Ground Black Pepper
1 jar (4 ounces) diced pimiento, drained
   (optional)
1 can (2.8 ounces) DURKEE French Fried
   Onions

Preheat oven to 350°. In large bowl, combine
vegetables, soup, *½ cup* cheese, the sour cream,
pepper, pimiento and *½ can* French Fried Onions.
Pour into shallow 1-quart casserole. Bake,
covered, at 350° for 30 minutes or until
vegetables are done. Sprinkle remaining cheese
and onions in diagonal rows across top; bake,
uncovered, 5 minutes or until onions are golden
brown.

Preparation time: 5 minutes

Microwave Directions: Prepare vegetable
mixture as above; pour into shallow 1-quart
microwave-safe casserole. Cook, covered, on
HIGH 8 to 10 minutes or until vegetables are
done. Stir vegetables halfway through cooking
time. Top with remaining cheese and onions as
above; cook, uncovered, 1 minute or until cheese
melts. Let stand 5 minutes.

■ Original Green Bean Casserole

Makes 6 servings

2 cans (16 ounces *each*) cut green beans,
   drained, or 2 packages (9 ounces *each*)
   frozen cut green beans, cooked and
   drained
¾ cup milk
1 can (10¾ ounces) condensed cream of
   mushroom soup
⅛ teaspoon DURKEE Ground Black Pepper
1 can (2.8 ounces) DURKEE French Fried
   Onions

Preheat oven to 350°. In medium bowl, combine
beans, milk, soup, pepper and *½ can* French Fried
Onions; pour into 1½-quart casserole. Bake,
uncovered, at 350° for 30 minutes or until heated
through. Top with remaining onions; bake,
uncovered, 5 minutes or until onions are golden
brown.

Preparation time: 5 minutes

Microwave Directions: Prepare green bean
mixture as above; pour into 1½-quart microwave-
safe casserole. Cook, covered, on HIGH 8 to 10
minutes or until heated through. Stir beans
halfway through cooking time. Top with
remaining onions; cook, uncovered, 1 minute. Let
stand 5 minutes.

*Top: **Original Green Bean Casserole;**
bottom: **Swiss Vegetable Medley***

■ Savory Sausage Dressing

Makes 6 to 8 servings

1 package (12 ounces) seasoned bulk pork
   sausage
¼ cup CRISCO® Oil
½ cup chopped onion
½ cup chopped celery
1 clove garlic, minced
1½ cups sliced fresh mushrooms
½ teaspoon Worcestershire sauce
¼ teaspoon dried rosemary leaves
⅛ teaspoon pepper
2 cups herb-seasoned stuffing mix
1 egg, slightly beaten
½ cup hot water
1½ teaspoons instant chicken bouillon
   granules

Preheat oven to 325°F. Place sausage in large
skillet. Cook over medium-high heat until no
longer pink. Drain. Transfer to medium mixing
bowl.

Heat CRISCO Oil in large skillet. Add onion,
celery and garlic. Sauté over moderate heat until
celery is tender-crisp. Add mushrooms,
Worcestershire sauce, rosemary and pepper.
Cook, stirring constantly, 1 minute. Add to
sausage. Mix well. Stir in stuffing mix and egg.
Mix hot water and bouillon granules in small
bowl. Stir into stuffing mixture. Place in 1½-quart
casserole. Bake at 325°F, 30 to 35 minutes, or
until heated through.

Savory Sausage Dressing

■ Cherry Cheese Mold

Makes 4 cups or 8 servings

1 can (8 ounces) dark sweet pitted cherries
1 package (4-serving size) JELL-O® Brand
   Cherry Flavor Gelatin
1½ cups crushed ice
2 packages (3 ounces each) cream cheese,
   softened and cut up

Drain cherries, reserving syrup. Add water to
syrup to make ¾ cup. Pour into small saucepan.
Bring to a boil over high heat. Pour boiling liquid
into blender. Add gelatin. Cover and blend at low
speed until gelatin is completely dissolved, about
30 seconds. Add crushed ice and cream cheese.
Blend at high speed for 1 minute. Pour into 4-cup
mold or bowl or individual dessert dishes. Drop
cherries into gelatin mixture, one at a time. Chill
until firm, about 1 hour. Unmold.

■ Golden Mashed Potatoes

Makes 4 to 6 servings

2½ cups cubed cooked potatoes, mashed
3 tablespoons milk
2 tablespoons PARKAY Margarine
1 tablespoon chopped fresh chives
½ lb. VELVEETA Pasteurized Process Cheese
   Spread, cubed
¼ cup (1 oz.) KRAFT 100% Grated Parmesan
   Cheese

Combine potatoes, milk, margarine and chives;
beat until fluffy. Stir in half of the process cheese
spread. Spoon into 1-quart casserole; sprinkle
with parmesan cheese. Bake at 350°, 20 to 25
minutes or until thoroughly heated. Top with
remaining process cheese spread; continue baking
until process cheese spread begins to melt.

Preparation time: 20 minutes

Baking time: 30 minutes

Cherry Waldorf Gelatin

■ Cherry Waldorf Gelatin

Makes 8 to 10 servings

2 cups boiling water
1 (6-ounce) package cherry flavor gelatin
1 cup cold water
¼ cup REALEMON® Lemon Juice from
    Concentrate
1½ cups chopped apples
1 cup chopped celery
½ cup chopped walnuts or pecans
    Lettuce leaves
    Apple slices and celery leaves, optional

In medium bowl, pour boiling water over gelatin; stir until dissolved. Add cold water and ReaLemon® brand; chill until partially set. Fold in apples, celery and nuts. Pour into lightly oiled 6-cup mold or 9-inch square baking pan. Chill until set, 4 to 6 hours or overnight. Serve on lettuce. Garnish with apple and celery leaves if desired.

■ Ambrosia

Makes 4 servings

1 can (20 ounces) DOLE® Pineapple Chunks
1 can (11 ounces) DOLE® Mandarin Orange
    Segments
1 firm, large DOLE® Banana, sliced, optional
1½ cups DOLE® Seedless Grapes
1 cup miniature marshmallows
1 cup flaked coconut
½ cup pecan halves or coarsely chopped nuts
1 cup dairy sour cream or plain yogurt
1 tablespoon brown sugar

Drain pineapple and orange segments. In large bowl, combine pineapple, orange segments, banana, grapes, marshmallows, coconut and nuts. In 1-quart measure, combine sour cream and brown sugar. Stir into fruit mixture. Refrigerate, covered, 1 hour or overnight.

■ Vegetables in Cheese Sauce

Makes about 5½ cups or 8 servings

> 1 can (11 ounces) CAMPBELL'S Condensed
>   Cheddar Cheese Soup/Sauce
> ⅓ cup milk
> ½ teaspoon dried basil leaves, crushed
> 1 clove garlic, minced
> 2 cups cauliflowerets
> 1 small onion, cut into thin wedges
> 1½ cups diagonally sliced carrots
> 1 package (10 ounces) frozen peas

1. In 3-quart microwave-safe casserole, stir soup until smooth. Stir in milk, basil and garlic; mix well.

2. Add vegetables; stir to coat well. Cover with lid; microwave on HIGH 15 minutes or until vegetables are tender, stirring twice during cooking. Let stand, covered, 5 minutes.

■ Winter Fruit Bowl

Makes about 6½ cups or 12 servings

> 2 packages (4-serving size) or 1 package
>   (8-serving size) JELL-O® Brand Lemon
>   Flavor Gelatin
> 1½ cups boiling water
> 1 can (12 fluid ounces) lemon-lime
>   carbonated beverage, chilled
>   Ice cubes
> 3 cups diced or sliced fresh fruits* (bananas,
>   oranges, apples, pears, grapes)

Dissolve gelatin in boiling water. Combine beverage and ice cubes to make 2½ cups. Add to gelatin, stirring until slightly thickened. Remove any unmelted ice. Chill until thickened, about 10 minutes. Fold in fruits. Pour into 8-cup serving bowl. Chill until set, about 3 hours. Garnish with whipped topping and orange sections, if desired.

Do not use fresh pineapple, kiwifruit, mango, papaya or figs.

■ Christmas Ribbon

Makes about 6 cups or 12 servings

> 2 packages (4-serving size) or 1 package
>   (8-serving size) JELL-O® Brand
>   Strawberry Flavor Gelatin
> 5 cups boiling water
> ⅔ cup sour cream or vanilla yogurt
> 2 packages (4-serving size) or 1 package
>   (8-serving size) JELL-O® Brand Lime
>   Flavor Gelatin

Dissolve strawberry flavor gelatin in 2½ cups of the boiling water. Pour 1½ cups of the strawberry flavor gelatin into 6-cup ring mold. Chill until set but not firm, about 30 minutes. Chill remaining strawberry flavor gelatin in bowl until slightly thickened. Gradually blend in ⅓ cup of the sour cream. Spoon over gelatin in mold. Chill until set but not firm, about 15 minutes.

Dissolve lime flavor gelatin in remaining boiling water. Chill until slightly thickened. Pour 1½ cups of the lime flavor gelatin over creamy layer in mold. Chill until set but not firm, about 15 minutes. Chill remaining lime flavor gelatin in bowl until slightly thickened. Gradually blend in remaining sour cream. Spoon over gelatin in mold. Chill about 2 hours. Unmold.

■ Home-Style Creamed Corn Casserole

Makes 6 servings

> 2 cans (17 oz. each) cream-style corn
> 1 cup MINUTE® Rice
> 1 egg, slightly beaten
> ½ teaspoon salt
> ⅛ teaspoon pepper
> ⅛ teaspoon ground nutmeg

Combine all ingredients in large bowl; mix well. Pour into greased 9-inch square baking dish. Bake at 375° for 25 minutes or until liquid is absorbed. Garnish as desired. Makes 6 servings.

Microwave Directions: Combine all ingredients in large bowl; mix well. Pour into greased 9-inch square microwavable dish. Cover with plastic wrap and cook at HIGH 15 minutes or until liquid is absorbed. Garnish as desired.

Vegetables in Cheese Sauce

■ Holiday Stuffing & Potato Bake

Makes 4 to 6 servings

1½ cups water
¼ cup butter or margarine
1 package (6 ounces) corn bread stuffing mix*
1 cup chopped apple
½ cup chopped celery
1 egg, beaten
1 can (2.8 ounces) DURKEE French Fried Onions
3 cups hot mashed potatoes
1 cup (4 ounces) shredded Cheddar cheese

Preheat oven to 350°. In large saucepan, heat water and butter until butter melts; remove from heat. Stir in both pouches of stuffing mix, apple, celery, egg and ½ *can* French Fried Onions; mix well. Set aside. To hot mashed potatoes, add ½ *cup* Cheddar cheese; stir. In greased 8×12-inch baking dish, make 4 alternating rows of potatoes and stuffing. Bake, covered, at 350° for 30 minutes or until heated through. Sprinkle remaining cheese and onions between each row of stuffing and potatoes; bake, uncovered, 5 minutes or until onions are golden brown.

*3 cups corn bread stuffing crumbs may be substituted for stuffing mix. Substitute 1 cup chicken broth for the water.

Preparation time: 15 minutes

Microwave Directions: In medium microwave-safe bowl, place water and butter. Cook, covered, on HIGH 3 minutes or until butter melts. Stir in stuffing ingredients as above. Prepare potato mixture as above. In 8×12-inch microwave-safe dish, arrange stuffing and potatoes as above. Cook, covered, 8 to 10 minutes or until heated through. Rotate dish halfway through cooking time. Top with remaining cheese and onions as above; cook, uncovered, 1 minute or until cheese melts. Let stand 5 minutes.

■ Broccoli and Rice with Walnuts

Makes 4 servings

¼ cup coarsely chopped walnuts or slivered almonds
1 tablespoon oil
½ package (2¼ cups) BIRDS EYE® Broccoli Cuts*
2 tablespoons sliced scallions
1 garlic clove, minced
1 cup chicken broth or water
2 tablespoons dry sherry (optional)
1½ tablespoons soy sauce
1 cup MINUTE® Rice

Cook and stir walnuts in hot oil in large skillet until lightly browned; remove from skillet. Add broccoli, scallions and garlic to oil remaining in skillet. Cook and stir 2 to 3 minutes. Add broth, sherry and soy sauce. Bring to a full boil. Stir in rice. Cover; remove from heat. Let stand 5 minutes. Fluff with fork and sprinkle with walnuts.

*You may use 1 package (9 oz.) BIRDS EYE® Cut Green Beans for the broccoli.

■ Easy Oyster Dressing

Makes 6 to 8 servings

1 teaspoon WYLER'S® or STEERO® Chicken-Flavor Instant Bouillon
½ cup boiling water
½ cup chopped celery
½ cup margarine or butter
1 (8-ounce) package herb-seasoned stuffing mix
1 (8-ounce) can ORLEANS® Whole Oysters, undrained

Preheat oven to 350°. Dissolve bouillon in water; set aside. In small skillet, cook celery in margarine until tender. In large bowl, combine all ingredients; mix well. Turn into buttered 1½-quart baking dish. Cover; bake 35 minutes or until hot. Refrigerate leftovers.

Ginger Pineapple Mold

■ Ginger Pineapple Mold

Makes 5 cups or 10 servings

    1 can (20 ounces) pineapple slices in juice
    2 packages (4-serving size) or 1 package
      (8-serving size) JELL-O® Brand Lime or
      Apricot Flavor Gelatin
 1½ cups boiling water
    1 cup ginger ale or cold water
    ¼ teaspoon ginger

Drain pineapple, reserving juice. Cut 4 pineapple slices in half; set aside. Cut remaining pineapple slices into chunks. Dissolve gelatin in boiling water. Add reserved juice, ginger ale and ginger. Chill until slightly thickened. Measure 1 cup of the gelatin. Arrange some of the pineapple chunks in 6-cup ring mold; top with measured gelatin. Chill until set but not firm, about 10 minutes. Fold remaining pineapple chunks into remaining gelatin; spoon over gelatin in mold. Chill until firm, about 4 hours. Unmold. Garnish with halved pineapple slices, halved cherry tomatoes and crisp greens, if desired.

■ Cranberry Waldorf Fluff

Makes 6 servings

 1½ cups cranberries, finely chopped
    1 cup KRAFT Miniature Marshmallows
    ¼ cup sugar
 1½ cups finely chopped apple
    ½ cup MIRACLE WHIP Salad Dressing
    ¼ cup chopped walnuts
    ⅛ teaspoon ground cinnamon

Combine cranberries, miniature marshmallows and sugar; mix lightly. Cover; chill. Add remaining ingredients; mix lightly.

Preparation time: 20 minutes plus chilling

■ Holiday Waldorf Salad

Makes about 7 cups or 14 servings

> 2 packages (4-serving size) or 1 package
> (8-serving size) JELL-O® Brand
> Strawberry Flavor Gelatin
> 1½ cups boiling water
> 1 tablespoon lemon juice
> 1 cup cold water
> Ice cubes
> 1 medium red apple, diced
> ½ cup halved seedless grapes
> ½ cup thinly sliced celery
> ½ cup chopped walnuts
> 1 cup mayonnaise

Completely dissolve gelatin in boiling water; add lemon juice. Combine cold water and ice cubes to make 2½ cups. Add to gelatin, stirring until slightly thickened. Remove any unmelted ice. Chill until thickened, about 10 minutes. Fold in apple, grapes, celery and nuts. Measure 1 cup of the gelatin and set aside. Pour remaining gelatin into 8-cup bowl. Chill until set but not firm.

Blend mayonnaise into measured gelatin. Spoon over fruited layer in bowl. Chill until set, about 3 hours. Garnish with fresh fruit and crisp greens, if desired.

■ Pineapple Cranberry Relish

Makes 4 cups

> 1 can (8¼ oz.) DOLE® Crushed Pineapple in
> Syrup
> 1 large thin-skinned navel orange, unpeeled
> 1 package (12 oz.) fresh cranberries, washed
> 1 cup sugar

Drain syrup from pineapple into blender. Cut orange into about 1-inch pieces; add to blender. Whir until pieces are coarse. Stop and stir as needed. Pour half of mixture from blender into a bowl. Add half of cranberries to blender; whir until coarsely chopped. Repeat with remaining cranberries and orange mixture. Pour all into a bowl; add pineapple and sugar. Cover with plastic wrap. Stand at room temperature overnight. Store in tightly covered jars in refrigerator.

Tip: Ripens and mellows when left on counter overnight.

■ Broccoli Casserole

Makes 6 to 8 servings

> 2 10-oz. pkgs. frozen chopped broccoli,
> thawed, drained
> 1½ cups cooked rice
> 1 10¾-oz. can condensed cream of
> mushroom soup
> ¾ lb. VELVEETA Pasteurized Process Cheese
> Spread, cubed
> 1 2.8-oz. can French fried onions

In large bowl, combine broccoli, rice, soup, process cheese spread and 1 cup onions; mix well. Spoon into 1½-quart casserole. Bake at 350°, 35 minutes. Top with remaining onions; continue baking 5 minutes.

Preparation time: 10 minutes

Baking time: 40 minutes

■ Apple-Cinnamon Sweet Potatoes

Serves 6

> 1 lb sweet potatoes, peeled (about
> 2 medium)
> 2 large apples, cored and sliced
> ¾ cup orange juice
> ¼ cup firmly packed brown sugar
> 1 Tbs lemon juice
> ½ tsp salt
> ½ tsp cinnamon
> 1 Tbs butter
> ½ cup chopped pecans

Grease a 1½ quart glass casserole. Thinly slice sweet potatoes and layer alternately with apples in prepared casserole. Mix orange juice, brown sugar, lemon juice, salt, and cinnamon. Pour over potatoes and apples. Cover and microwave on high power 5 minutes. Spoon sauce over, re-cover and microwave 5 minutes. Spoon sauce over again. Re-cover and continue microwaving on high power 5 to 6 minutes or until potatoes and apples are tender. Dot with butter and sprinkle with nuts. Microwave on high power, uncovered, 2 to 3 minutes. Let stand 5 minutes before serving.

Favorite Recipe from **Western New York Apple Growers Association, Inc.**

■ Wild Rice & Pepper Salad

Makes 6 servings

- 1 6-oz. pkg. long-grain & wild rice
- ½ cup MIRACLE WHIP Salad Dressing
- 2 tablespoons olive oil
- ½ teaspoon black pepper
- ¼ teaspoon grated lemon peel
- 1 cup chopped red pepper
- 1 cup chopped yellow pepper
- ¼ cup 1-inch green onion pieces

Prepare rice as directed on package, omitting margarine. Cool. Combine salad dressing, oil, black pepper and peel; mix well. Add remaining ingredients; mix lightly. Serve at room temperature or chilled.

Preparation time: 35 minutes

Variation: Substitute MIRACLE WHIP Light Reduced Calorie Salad Dressing for Regular Salad Dressing.

Wild Rice & Pepper Salad

■ Applesauce Cranberry Mold

Serves 6 to 8

- 2 envelopes plain gelatin
- ½ cup orange or cranberry juice
- ½ cup boiling water
- 1 can or jar (16 oz) cranberry sauce
- 1 cup applesauce
- 1 apple, cored and cut up
- 1 cup diced celery
- ½ cup chopped walnuts
- 1 orange, peeled and diced
- 2 Tbs grated orange rind

Soften gelatin in juice. Add boiling water; cool. Mix all other ingredients; add to gelatin mixture. Pour into a greased mold (at least 2 quarts) and refrigerate several hours.

Favorite Recipe from **Western New York Apple Growers Association, Inc.**

■ Sherried Mushroom Rice

Makes 4 servings

- 1 garlic clove, minced
- 2 tablespoons butter or margarine
- 2 cups sliced mushrooms
- ¼ cup chopped red pepper
- 1¼ cups chicken broth
- ¼ cup dry sherry or chicken broth
- 2 teaspoons onion flakes
- ½ teaspoon salt
- 1½ cups MINUTE® Rice
- 2 tablespoons grated Parmesan cheese
- 1 tablespoon chopped parsley

Cook and stir garlic in hot butter in large skillet 1 minute. Add mushrooms and red pepper; cook, stirring occasionally, 2 minutes.

Add broth, sherry, onion flakes and salt. Bring to a full boil. Stir in rice. Cover; remove from heat. Let stand 5 minutes. Fluff with fork and sprinkle with grated cheese and parsley. Serve with steak or your favorite main dish. Garnish as desired.

Microwave Directions: Cut butter into pieces. Cook garlic, butter and mushrooms in microwavable dish at HIGH 2 to 3 minutes. Stir in remaining ingredients except Parmesan cheese and parsley. Cover and cook at HIGH 4 minutes. Stir; cover and cook at HIGH 2 to 3 minutes longer. Let stand 5 minutes. Fluff with fork and sprinkle with Parmesan cheese and parsley. Serve with steak or your favorite main dish.

■ Cranberry Holiday Ring

Makes 12 servings

- 2¼ cups cold water
- 1 3-oz. pkg. strawberry flavored gelatin
- 1 10½-oz. can frozen cranberry-orange relish, thawed
- 1 8-oz. can crushed pineapple
- 1 3-oz. pkg. lemon flavored gelatin
- 2 cups KRAFT Miniature Marshmallows
- ½ cup MIRACLE WHIP Salad Dressing
- 1 cup whipping cream, whipped

Bring 1 cup water to boil. Gradually add to strawberry gelatin, stirring until dissolved. Add cranberry-orange relish; mix well. Pour into lightly oiled 6½-cup ring mold; cover. Chill until almost set. Drain pineapple, reserving liquid. Bring remaining water to boil. Gradually add to lemon gelatin, stirring until dissolved. Add marshmallows; stir until melted. Add reserved pineapple liquid; cover. Chill until partially set. Add salad dressing and pineapple to marshmallow mixture. Fold in whipped cream; pour over strawberry layer. Cover; chill until firm. Unmold. Garnish as desired.

Preparation time: 1½ hours plus final chilling

Variation: Substitute 12×8-inch baking dish for ring mold. Do not unmold.

Sherried Mushroom Rice

■ Spinach Bake

Makes 8 servings

> 2 eggs, beaten
> ¾ cup MIRACLE WHIP Salad Dressing
> 2 10-oz. pkgs. frozen chopped spinach, thawed, well drained
> 1 14-oz. can artichoke hearts, drained, cut into quarters
> ½ cup sour cream
> ¼ cup (1 oz.) KRAFT 100% Grated Parmesan Cheese
> 6 crisply cooked bacon slices, crumbled

Combine eggs and ½ cup salad dressing, mixing until well blended. Add spinach and artichokes; mix lightly. Spoon mixture into lightly greased 10×6-inch baking dish. Combine remaining salad dressing, sour cream and cheese; mix well. Spoon over spinach mixture. Bake at 350°, 30 minutes or until set. Sprinkle with bacon.

Preparation time: 10 minutes

Baking time: 30 minutes

Microwave: Substitute 1½-quart microwave-safe casserole for 10×6-inch baking dish. Combine eggs and ½ cup salad dressing in casserole, mixing until well blended. Add spinach and artichokes; mix lightly. Microwave on High 8 to 9 minutes or until thoroughly heated, stirring every 3 minutes. Combine remaining salad dressing, sour cream and cheese; mix well. Spoon over spinach mixture. Microwave on High 1½ to 2 minutes or until sour cream mixture is warmed. (Do not over cook.) Sprinkle with bacon. Let stand 5 minutes.

Microwave tip: To thaw spinach, place frozen spinach in 1½-quart microwave-safe casserole; cover. Microwave on High 5 minutes. Break apart with fork; drain well.

■ Rich Turkey Gravy

Makes about 1½ cups

> ¼ to ⅓ cup unsifted flour
> ¼ cup turkey pan drippings *or* margarine
> 2 cups hot water
> 2 teaspoons WYLER'S® or STEERO® Chicken-Flavor Instant Bouillon *or* 2 Chicken-Flavor Bouillon Cubes

In medium skillet, stir flour into drippings until smooth; cook and stir until dark brown. Add water and bouillon; cook and stir until thickened and bouillon is dissolved. Refrigerate leftovers.

Holiday Fruit Salad

A colorful addition to a holiday buffet dinner.

■ Holiday Fruit Salad

Makes 12 servings

> 3 packages (3 ounces each) strawberry flavor gelatin
> 3 cups boiling water
> 2 ripe DOLE® Bananas
> 1 package (16 ounces) frozen strawberries
> 1 can (20 ounces) DOLE® Crushed Pineapple
> 1 package (8 ounces) cream cheese, softened
> 1 cup dairy sour cream or plain yogurt
> ¼ cup sugar
> Crisp DOLE® Lettuce leaves

In large bowl, dissolve gelatin in boiling water. Slice bananas into gelatin mixture. Add frozen strawberries and undrained pineapple. Pour half the mixture into 13×9-inch pan. Refrigerate 1 hour or until firm. In mixer bowl, beat cream cheese with sour cream and sugar; spread over chilled layer. Gently spoon remaining gelatin mixture on top. Refrigerate until firm, about 2 hours. Cut into squares; serve on lettuce-lined salad plates. Garnish with additional pineapple, if desired.

Fresh Vegetable Ring

■ Fresh Vegetable Ring

Makes 6 servings

2 cups broccoli flowerets
2 cups cauliflowerets
1 small zucchini, cut into ¼-inch slices
1 small yellow squash, cut into ¼-inch slices
1 can (10¾ ounces) CAMPBELL'S® Condensed
   Chicken Broth
6 medium CAMPBELL'S® Fresh Mushrooms,
   halved
   Sweet red pepper strips for garnish
2 teaspoons cornstarch
1 teaspoon chopped fresh basil leaves or
   ½ teaspoon dried basil leaves, crushed
1 teaspoon wine vinegar

1. Arrange broccoli in a circle around rim of a 12-inch round microwave-safe platter. Arrange cauliflower next to broccoli. Arrange alternate slices of zucchini and yellow squash next to cauliflower, leaving space in center of platter. Pour ¼ cup of the broth over vegetables. Cover with vented plastic wrap; microwave on HIGH 5 minutes.

2. Place mushrooms in center of platter. Garnish with red pepper strips. Cover; microwave on HIGH 2 minutes or until vegetables are tender-crisp. Let stand, covered, while preparing sauce.

3. In small microwave-safe bowl, blend remaining broth, cornstarch, basil and vinegar until smooth. Cover with vented plastic wrap; microwave on HIGH 2 minutes or until mixture boils, stirring twice during cooking. Spoon over vegetables.

Parmesan Potato Crisp

Makes 6 servings

½ cup MIRACLE WHIP Salad Dressing
5 cups thin unpeeled potato slices
¾ cup (3 ozs.) KRAFT 100% Grated Parmesan
   Cheese
Pepper (optional)

Generously brush 9-inch pie plate with salad dressing. Dry potato slices on paper towel. Arrange one layer of potatoes, edges slightly overlapping, on bottom of pie plate. Brush generously with salad dressing; sprinkle generously with cheese. Repeat layers, sprinkling occasionally with pepper. Bake at 400°, 30 minutes. Cover with foil; continue baking 30 minutes or until potatoes are tender. Immediately invert onto serving plate. Cut into wedges to serve.

Preparation time: 10 minutes

Baking time: 1 hour

Variation: Substitute MIRACLE WHIP Light Reduced Calorie Salad Dressing for Regular Salad Dressing.

If desired, leave the peels on the potatoes for a more homey casserole.

Potato and Cheese Casserole

Makes 6 servings

1 can (10¾ ounces) CAMPBELL'S® Condensed
   Cream of Celery Soup
1 cup shredded Cheddar cheese (4 ounces)
½ cup milk
   Generous dash pepper
1 large clove garlic, minced
4 cups thinly sliced potatoes
1 cup thinly sliced onions

1. In medium bowl, stir soup until smooth. Add cheese, milk, pepper and garlic; stir until well blended.

2. In 2-quart microwave-safe casserole, arrange ½ of the potatoes, ½ of the onions and ½ of the soup mixture. Repeat layers.

3. Cover with lid; microwave on HIGH 23 minutes or until potatoes are tender, rotating dish 3 times during cooking. Let stand, covered, 5 minutes.

Festive Rice

Makes 6 servings

2¼ cups MINUTE® Rice
1 medium green pepper, chopped*
¼ cup oil
1 envelope GOOD SEASONS® Italian or Mild
   Italian Salad Dressing Mix
2¼ cups water
2 tablespoons chopped pimiento or parsley

Cook and stir rice and green pepper in hot oil in large skillet about 2 minutes. Sprinkle with salad dressing mix. Stir in water. Cover and bring to a boil. Remove from heat. Let stand 5 minutes. Stir in pimiento.

You may use ½ medium green pepper, chopped, and ½ cup grated carrot for the green pepper.

Raspberry-Lemon Gelatin Salad

Makes 8 to 10 servings

1 10-oz. pkg. frozen raspberries, thawed
   Cold water
1 3-oz. pkg. raspberry flavored gelatin
1 envelope unflavored gelatin
½ cup lemon juice
1 3½-oz. pkg. lemon instant pudding and pie
   filling mix
2 cups cold milk
1 cup MIRACLE WHIP Salad Dressing

Drain raspberries, reserving liquid. Add enough water to reserved liquid to measure ¾ cup; set aside. Bring 1 cup water to boil. Gradually add to raspberry flavored gelatin, stirring until dissolved. Stir in reserved raspberry liquid. Cover; chill until thickened but not set. Fold in raspberries. Pour into 1½-quart clear serving bowl. Cover; chill until almost set. Combine unflavored gelatin and juice in small saucepan; let stand 1 minute. Stir over low heat until gelatin is dissolved. Cool. Combine pudding mix and milk; mix as directed on package for pudding. Stir in salad dressing. Gradually add gelatin mixture, mixing until well blended. Pour over raspberry layer; cover. Chill until firm.

Preparation time: 1½ hours plus final chilling

Main Dishes

■ Turkey with Apple Citrus Stuffing

Makes 10 to 12 servings (8 cups stuffing)

12- to 14-pound BUTTERBALL® Turkey, thawed
    if frozen
1 cup chopped celery
½ cup chopped onion
6 tablespoons margarine or butter
2 teaspoons poultry seasoning
8 cups slightly dried bread cubes
    (10 to 12 bread slices, cubed and dried
    overnight)
2 cups chopped red apple
¼ cup chopped fresh parsley
1½ teaspoons shredded orange peel
    Juice from orange plus water to make
      ¾ cup

Cook and stir celery and onion in margarine in medium saucepan over medium heat until crisp-tender. Stir in poultry seasoning. Combine bread cubes, apple, parsley and orange peel in large bowl. Add celery mixture and orange juice mixture; toss to mix. Preheat oven to 325°F. Prepare turkey for roasting; stuff neck and body cavities lightly. Roast immediately according to package directions.

■ Holiday Baked Ham

Makes 8 to 10 servings

1 bone-in smoked ham (8½ pounds)
1 can (20 ounces) DOLE® Sliced Pineapple in
    Syrup
1 cup apricot preserves
1 teaspoon dry mustard
½ teaspoon ground allspice
    Whole cloves
    Maraschino cherries

Preheat oven to 325°F. Remove rind from ham. Place ham on rack in open roasting pan, fat side up. Insert meat thermometer with bulb in thickest part away from fat or bone. Roast ham in oven about 3 hours.

Drain pineapple; reserve syrup. In small saucepan, combine syrup, preserves, mustard and allspice. Bring to boil; boil, stirring occasionally, 10 minutes. Remove ham from oven, but keep oven hot. Stud ham with cloves; brush with glaze. Using wooden picks, secure pineapple and cherries to ham. Brush again with glaze. Return ham to oven. Roast 30 minutes longer or until thermometer registers 160°F (about 25 minutes per pound total cooking time). Brush with glaze 15 minutes before done. Let ham stand 20 minutes before slicing.

Turkey with Apple Citrus Stuffing

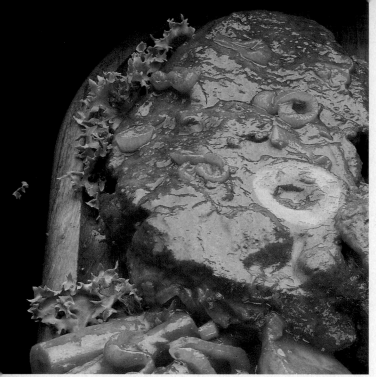

Savory Pot Roast

■ Savory Pot Roast

Makes 4 servings

6 tablespoons all-purpose flour, divided
1 teaspoon celery salt
1 teaspoon dried marjoram leaves
½ teaspoon dried summer savory leaves
⅛ teaspoon pepper
3½- to 4-pound beef chuck roast
¼ cup CRISCO® Oil
1 medium onion, thinly sliced
½ cup water
1 can (8 ounces) tomato sauce
2 teaspoons instant beef bouillon granules
4 medium carrots, cut into 3-inch pieces
4 medium potatoes, quartered
¼ cup cold water

Mix 4 tablespoons flour, celery salt, marjoram, summer savory and pepper in shallow baking dish. Coat roast evenly with flour mixture. Heat CRISCO Oil in Dutch oven. Add roast and any remaining flour mixture. Brown over medium-high heat. Add onion, ½ cup water, tomato sauce and bouillon granules. Cover. Reduce heat. Simmer about 2 hours. Add carrots and potatoes; re-cover. Simmer about 1 hour, or until vegetables are tender. Transfer roast and vegetables to serving platter, reserving cooking liquid in Dutch oven.

Place ¼ cup cold water in 1-cup measure or small bowl. Mix in remaining 2 tablespoons flour. Stir into reserved cooking liquid. Cook over medium-high heat, stirring constantly, until thickened and bubbly. Serve with beef and vegetables.

■ Turkey Tetrazzini

Makes 6 servings

⅔ cup MIRACLE WHIP Salad Dressing
⅓ cup flour
½ teaspoon celery salt
   Dash of pepper
2 cups milk
7 ozs. spaghetti, broken into thirds, cooked, drained
2 cups chopped cooked turkey or chicken
¾ cup (3 ozs.) KRAFT 100% Grated Parmesan Cheese
1 4-oz. can mushrooms drained
2 tablespoons chopped pimento (optional)
2 cups fresh bread cubes
3 tablespoons PARKAY Margarine, melted

Combine salad dressing, flour and seasonings in medium saucepan. Gradually add milk. Cook, stirring constantly, over low heat until thickened. Add spaghetti, turkey, ½ cup cheese, mushrooms and pimento; mix lightly. Spoon into 2-quart casserole. Toss bread cubes with margarine and remaining cheese; top casserole. Bake at 350°, 30 minutes or until lightly browned.

Preparation time: 30 minutes

Baking time: 30 minutes

Make ahead: Prepare as directed except for topping with bread cubes and baking. Cover; chill. When ready to bake, toss bread cubes with margarine and remaining cheese. Top casserole; cover with foil. Bake at 350°, 25 minutes. Uncover; continue baking 30 minutes or until lightly browned.

Microwave: Reduce margarine to 2 tablespoons. Microwave margarine in 2-quart microwave-safe casserole on High 30 seconds or until melted. Add bread cubes; toss. Microwave on High 3½ to 4½ minutes or until crisp, stirring after 2 minutes. Remove from casserole; set aside. Combine salad dressing, flour and seasonings in same casserole; gradually add milk. Microwave on High 5 to 6 minutes or until thickened, stirring after each minute. Stir in spaghetti, turkey, ½ cup cheese, mushrooms and pimento; mix lightly. Cover; microwave on High 8 to 10 minutes or until thoroughly heated, stirring after 5 minutes. Stir; top with bread cubes. Sprinkle with remaining cheese. Let stand 5 minutes.

■ Fried Chicken

4 servings

⅓ cup all-purpose flour
½ teaspoon salt
½ teaspoon paprika
¼ teaspoon garlic powder
¼ teaspoon pepper
1 can (5.3 ounces) evaporated milk
1 broiler-fryer chicken (2½ to 3 pounds), cut up
¼ cup CRISCO® Oil

Mix flour, salt, paprika, garlic powder and pepper in large plastic food storage bag. Set aside. Pour evaporated milk into bowl. Dip chicken in evaporated milk. Add a few chicken pieces to food storage bag. Shake to coat. Remove chicken from bag. Repeat with remaining chicken.

Heat CRISCO Oil in large skillet. Add chicken. Brown over medium-high heat. Cook over moderate heat about 25 minutes, or until meat near bone is no longer pink and juices run clear, turning pieces over frequently.

Fried Chicken

■ Simple Shrimp Creole

Makes about 5 cups or 4 servings

1 tablespoon butter or margarine
½ cup chopped onion
1 medium green pepper, cut into matchstick-thin strips
½ cup thinly sliced celery
1 jar (15 ounces) PREGO® al Fresco Spaghetti Sauce
¾ pound medium shrimp, shelled and deveined
1 bay leaf
⅛ teaspoon pepper
  Generous dash hot pepper sauce
  Hot cooked rice

1. In 2-quart microwave-safe casserole, combine butter, onion, green pepper and celery. Cover with lid; microwave on HIGH 4 minutes or until vegetables are tender, stirring once during cooking.

2. Stir in spaghetti sauce, shrimp, bay leaf, pepper and hot pepper sauce. Cover; microwave on HIGH 6 minutes or until shrimp are opaque, stirring once during cooking. Remove bay leaf. Serve over rice.

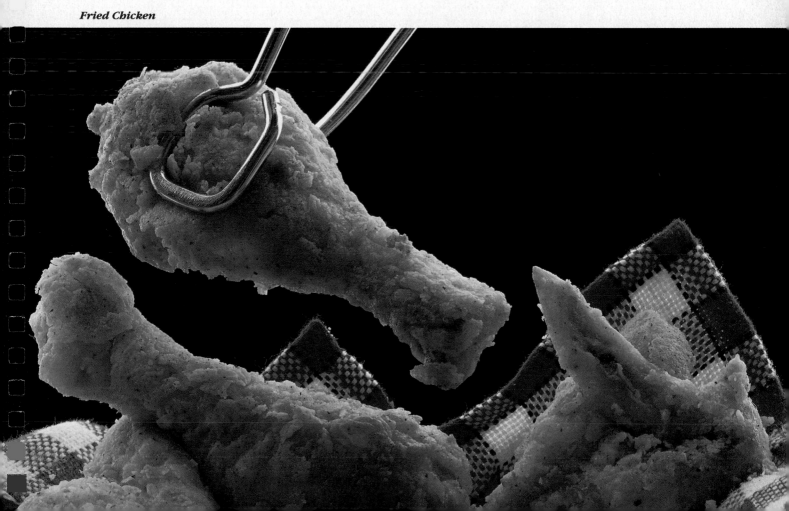

■ Tasty Turkey Pot Pie

Makes 4 to 6 servings

- ½ cup MIRACLE WHIP Salad Dressing
- 2 tablespoons flour
- 1 teaspoon instant chicken bouillon
- ⅛ teaspoon pepper
- ¾ cup milk
- 1½ cups chopped cooked turkey or chicken
- 1 10-oz. pkg. frozen mixed vegetables, thawed, drained
- 1 4-oz. can refrigerated quick crescent dinner rolls

Combine salad dressing, flour, bouillon and pepper in medium saucepan. Gradually add milk. Cook, stirring constantly, over low heat until thickened. Add turkey and vegetables; heat thoroughly, stirring occasionally. Spoon into 8-inch square baking dish. Unroll dough into two rectangles. Press perforations together to seal. Place rectangles side-by-side to form square; press edges together to form seam. Cover turkey mixture with dough. Bake at 375°, 15 to 20 minutes or until browned.

Preparation time: 15 minutes

Baking time: 20 minutes

Variations: Combine 1 egg, beaten, and 1 tablespoon cold water, mixing until well blended. Brush dough with egg mixture just before baking.

Substitute one chicken bouillon cube for instant chicken bouillon.

Substitute 10×6-inch baking dish for 8-inch square baking dish.

Substitute 12×8-inch baking dish for 8-inch square dish. Double all ingredients. Assemble recipe as directed, using three dough rectangles to form top crust. Decorate crust with cut-outs from remaining rectangle. Bake as directed.

Microwave tip: To prepare sauce, combine salad dressing, flour, bouillon and pepper in 1-quart microwave-safe measure or bowl; gradually add milk. Microwave on High 4 to 5 minutes or until thickened, stirring after each minute.

■ Oven-Baked Bourguignonne

Makes about 8 servings

- 2 pounds boneless beef chuck, cut into 1-inch cubes
- ¼ cup all-purpose flour
- 1⅓ cups sliced carrots
- 1 can (14½ ounces) whole peeled tomatoes, undrained and chopped
- 1 bay leaf
- 1 envelope LIPTON® Beefy Onion or Onion Recipe Soup Mix
- ½ cup dry red wine
- 1 cup fresh or canned sliced mushrooms
- 1 package (8 ounces) medium or broad egg noodles

Preheat oven to 400°.

In 2-quart casserole, toss beef with flour, then bake uncovered 20 minutes. Add carrots, tomatoes and bay leaf, then beefy onion recipe soup mix blended with wine. Bake covered 1½ hours or until beef is tender. Add mushrooms and bake covered an additional 10 minutes. Remove bay leaf.

Meanwhile, cook noodles according to package directions. To serve, arrange bourguignonne over noodles.

Microwave Directions: Toss beef with flour; set aside. In 2-quart casserole, combine tomatoes, bay leaf and beefy onion recipe soup mix blended with wine. Heat covered at HIGH (Full Power) 7 minutes, stirring once. Add beef and carrots. Heat covered at DEFROST (30% Full Power), stirring occasionally, 1¼ hours. Add mushrooms and heat covered at DEFROST 30 minutes or until beef is tender. Remove bay leaf. Let stand covered 5 minutes. Cook noodles and serve as above.

Freezing/Reheating Directions: Bourguignonne can be baked, then frozen. Simply wrap covered casserole in heavy-duty aluminum foil; freeze. To reheat, unwrap and bake covered at 400°, stirring occasionally to separate beef and vegetables, 1 hour. OR, microwave at HIGH (Full Power), stirring occasionally, 20 minutes or until heated through. Let stand covered 5 minutes.

Curried Turkey Dinner

■ Curried Turkey Dinner

Serves 4

> 1 Package (10 oz.) frozen broccoli spears, cooked and drained
> 2 Cups COOKED TURKEY, cubed
> 1 Can (10½ oz.) reduced-sodium cream of mushroom soup
> ¼ Cup reduced-calorie mayonnaise
> 1½ Teaspoons lemon juice
> 1 Teaspoon curry powder
> 1 Cup seasoned croutons

1. Preheat oven to 350 degrees F.

2. In an 8-inch square baking dish layer broccoli; top with turkey.

3. In a small bowl combine soup, mayonnaise, lemon juice, and curry powder. Pour over turkey and top with croutons.

4. Bake 20 to 25 minutes or until bubbly.

APPROXIMATE NUTRIENT CONTENT PER SERVING: 321 KCAL; 24 gm protein; 16 gm fat; 21 gm carbohydrate; 720 mg sodium; 63 mg cholesterol.

Favorite Recipe from **National Turkey Federation**

■ Meat Loaf Italiano

Makes 6 servings

> 1 egg, beaten
> 1½ lbs. ground beef
> 1 8-oz. can pizza sauce
> ¾ cup (3 ozs.) VELVEETA Shredded Pasteurized Process Cheese Food
> ¾ cup old fashioned or quick oats, uncooked
> ¼ cup cold water
> ½ teaspoon dried oregano leaves, crushed

In large bowl, combine all ingredients except ¼ cup sauce; mix lightly. Shape into loaf in 10×6-inch baking dish. Bake at 350°, 1 hour. Top with remaining sauce. Let stand 10 minutes before serving.

Preparation time: 10 minutes

Baking time: 60 minutes plus standing

■ Standing Rib Roast with Madeira Sauce

Makes about 6 servings

- 2 large cloves garlic, finely chopped
- 1 teaspoon marjoram leaves (optional)
- 1 teaspoon thyme leaves
- 1 teaspoon salt
- ¼ teaspoon pepper
- 5- pound standing rib roast (about 3 ribs)
- ¼ cup butter or margarine
- 2 cups thinly sliced mushrooms
- ¼ cup Madeira or dry red wine
- 1 tablespoon tomato paste
- 1 envelope LIPTON® Onion, Onion-Mushroom or Beefy Mushroom Recipe Soup Mix
- 1 tablespoon all-purpose flour
- 1½ cups water
- 1 tablespoon finely chopped parsley
  Pepper to taste

Preheat oven to 500°. In small bowl, combine garlic, marjoram, thyme, salt and pepper; set aside.

Trim fat from roast. In roasting pan, on rack, place roast; rub with garlic mixture. Roast 10 minutes, then decrease heat to 350° and continue roasting 1½ hours or until meat thermometer reaches 130° (rare) or 150° (medium).

Remove roast to serving platter and keep warm. Skim fat from pan drippings. In medium saucepan, combine pan juices with butter; stir in mushrooms. Cook 5 minutes or until mushrooms are tender. Stir in wine and tomato paste, then onion recipe soup mix and flour blended with water. Bring to a boil, then simmer, stirring frequently, 5 minutes or until sauce is thickened. Stir in parsley and pepper. Serve sauce with roast.

■ Roasted Duckling with Orange & Plum Sauce

Makes about 2 servings

- 1 (3-pound) duckling
- 1 medium orange, halved
- 1 medium onion, halved
- ½ cup WISH-BONE® Deluxe French or Lite French-Style Dressing
- ½ cup orange juice
- 2 tablespoons brown sugar
- 1 teaspoon grated orange peel (optional)
- ¼ teaspoon ground cinnamon
- ⅛ teaspoon ground cloves
- ⅛ teaspoon ground nutmeg
- 1 tablespoon butter or margarine
- ½ cup chopped onion
- 1 teaspoon finely chopped garlic
- 2 tablespoons brandy
- 2 medium plums, pitted and cut into wedges
- 2 small oranges, peeled, sectioned and seeded

Preheat oven to 400°.

Stuff duckling with orange and onion halves. Close cavity with skewers or wooden toothpicks; tie legs together with string. With pin or fork, pierce skin. In roasting pan, on rack, place duckling breast side up. Roast 40 minutes, turning duckling every 10 minutes.

Meanwhile, in small bowl, blend deluxe French dressing, orange juice, sugar, orange peel, cinnamon, cloves and nutmeg. Pour ½ of the dressing mixture over duckling; loosely cover with heavy-duty aluminum foil. Continue roasting, basting occasionally, 30 minutes or until meat thermometer reaches 185°. Remove to serving platter and keep warm.

Meanwhile, in medium saucepan, melt butter and cook onion with garlic over medium heat, stirring occasionally, 5 minutes or until onion is tender. Add brandy, then plums and orange sections and cook, stirring occasionally, 5 minutes. Stir in remaining dressing mixture and heat through. Serve with duckling.

Turkey Cranberry Croissant

■ Turkey Cranberry Croissant

Yield: 6 sandwiches

Thin-sliced cooked BUTTERBALL® turkey
(1 pound)
1 package (8 ounces) cream cheese, softened
¼ cup orange marmalade
½ cup chopped pecans
6 croissants or rolls, split
¾ cup whole berry cranberry sauce
Lettuce leaves

Combine cream cheese, marmalade and pecans in
small bowl. Spread top and bottom halves of
croissants with cream cheese mixture. Layer
turkey on bottom halves. Spoon 2 tablespoons
cranberry sauce over turkey. Add lettuce and
croissant top.

■ Lemon Broiled Fish

Makes 4 servings

½ cup margarine or butter, melted
¼ cup REALEMON® Lemon Juice from
Concentrate
2 cups fresh bread crumbs (about 4 slices)
1 tablespoon chopped parsley
½ teaspoon paprika
1 pound fish fillets, fresh or frozen, thawed

Combine margarine and ReaLemon® brand. In
medium bowl, combine bread crumbs, parsley
and ¼ *cup* of the lemon mixture. Add paprika to
remaining lemon mixture. Dip fish into paprika
mixture; broil until fish flakes with fork. Top with
bread crumb mixture. Return to broiler; heat
through. Refrigerate leftovers.

■ Lasagna Italiano

Makes 6 to 8 servings

1½ lbs. ground beef
½ cup chopped onion
1 14½-oz. can tomatoes, cut up
1 6-oz. can tomato paste
⅓ cup cold water
1 garlic clove, minced
1 teaspoon dried oregano leaves, crushed
¼ teaspoon pepper
6 ozs. lasagna noodles, cooked, drained
2 6-oz. pkgs. 100% Natural KRAFT Low Moisture Part-Skim Mozzarella Cheese Slices
½ lb. VELVEETA Pasteurized Process Cheese Spread, thinly sliced
½ cup (2 ozs.) KRAFT 100% Grated Parmesan Cheese

In large skillet, brown meat; drain. Add onions; cook until tender. Stir in tomatoes, tomato paste, water, garlic and seasonings. Cover; simmer 30 minutes. In 12×8-inch baking dish, layer half of noodles, meat sauce, mozzarella cheese, process cheese spread and parmesan cheese; repeat layers. Bake at 350°, 30 minutes. Let stand 10 minutes before serving.

Preparation time: 40 minutes

Baking time: 30 minutes plus standing

■ Cajun Baked Fish

Makes 3 to 4 servings

⅓ cup MIRACLE WHIP Salad Dressing
½ teaspoon ground cumin
½ teaspoon onion powder
¼ teaspoon ground red pepper
¼ teaspoon garlic powder
1 lb. fish fillets
½ cup crushed sesame crackers

Combine salad dressing and seasonings; mix well. Brush fish with salad dressing mixture; coat with crumbs. Place in greased shallow baking dish. Bake at 350°, 30 minutes or until fish begins to flake when tested with a fork. Serve with your favorite accompaniments.

Preparation time: 15 minutes

Baking time: 30 minutes

Microwave: Combine salad dressing and seasonings; mix well. Brush fish with salad dressing mixture; coat with crumbs. Arrange fish in shallow microwave-safe baking dish, placing thickest portions toward outside of dish. Cover with plastic wrap; vent. Microwave on High 5 minutes, turning dish after 3 minutes. Let stand, covered, 2 to 3 minutes or until fish begins to flake when tested with a fork. Serve with your favorite accompaniments.

Fettuccine with Shrimp and Creamy Herb Sauce

Makes about 2 servings

1 envelope LIPTON® Creamy Herb Recipe
Soup Mix
1¾ cups milk
8 ounces frozen cleaned shrimp, partially
thawed*
½ cup frozen peas, partially thawed
6 ounces fettuccine or medium egg noodles,
cooked and drained
¼ cup grated Parmesan cheese

In 2-quart saucepan, with wire whip or fork,
thoroughly blend creamy herb recipe soup mix
with milk. Bring just to the boiling point, stirring
frequently. Add shrimp and peas and simmer 3
minutes or until shrimp are tender. Toss shrimp
sauce with hot noodles and cheese.

*Substitution: Use 8 ounces uncooked fresh
shrimp, cleaned.*

Microwave Directions: Decrease milk to 1¼
cups. In 2-quart casserole, with wire whip or fork,
thoroughly blend creamy herb recipe soup mix
with milk. Heat uncovered at HIGH (Full Power),
stirring occasionally, 5 minutes. Add shrimp and
peas and heat uncovered, stirring occasionally, 6
minutes or until shrimp are tender. Toss as above.

Italian Stuffed Shells

Makes 6 to 8 servings

24 CREAMETTE® Jumbo Macaroni Shells,
cooked and drained
1 pound lean ground beef
⅔ cup chopped onion
1 clove garlic, chopped
2 cups boiling water
1 (12-ounce) can tomato paste
1 tablespoon WYLER'S® Beef-Flavor Instant
Bouillon *or* 3 Beef-Flavor Bouillon Cubes
1½ teaspoons oregano leaves
1 (16-ounce) container BORDEN® or
MEADOW GOLD® Cottage Cheese
2 cups (8 ounces) shredded Mozzarella
cheese
½ cup grated Parmesan cheese
1 egg

In large skillet, brown beef, onion and garlic;
pour off fat. Stir in water, tomato paste, bouillon
and oregano; simmer 30 minutes. In medium
bowl, combine cottage cheese, *1 cup* Mozzarella,
grated Parmesan and egg; mix well. Stuff shells
with cheese mixture; arrange in individual
ramekins or 13×9-inch baking dish. Pour sauce
over shells; cover. Bake in preheated 350° oven
30 minutes. Uncover; sprinkle with remaining
1 cup Mozzarella. Bake 3 minutes longer.
Refrigerate leftovers.

Glazed Stuffed Cornish Hens

Makes 4 servings

2 (1½-pound) Cornish hens
¼ cup butter or margarine
½ cup chopped onion
½ cup sweet red pepper cut into julienne
strips
½ cup green pepper cut into julienne strips
4 cups herb-flavored stuffing mix
½ cup CAMPBELL'S® Condensed Chicken
Broth
½ cup water
½ cup apricot jam

1. Remove giblets and neck from inside hens
(reserve for another use if desired). Rinse hens;
pat dry. Split hens along backbone and
breastbone; set aside.

2. In 3-quart microwave-safe casserole, combine
butter, onion and peppers. Cover with vented
plastic wrap; microwave on HIGH 3 minutes or
until vegetables are tender, stirring once during
cooking. Add stuffing, broth and water; toss to
mix well.

3. Pat stuffing mixture into bottom of 12- by 8-
inch microwave-safe baking dish. Arrange hen
halves, skin-side up, over stuffing; set aside.

4. Place jam in small microwave-safe bowl.
Microwave, uncovered, on HIGH 45 seconds or
until melted. Brush jam over hens. Cover with
waxed paper; microwave on HIGH 17 minutes
or until hens are no longer pink in center,
rotating dish twice and rearranging hens once
during cooking. Let stand, covered, 5 minutes.

Desserts

■ Pumpkin Nut Pound Cake

Makes one 9×5-inch loaf

1¾ cups all-purpose flour
½ cup pecans, finely chopped or ground
1½ teaspoons ground cinnamon
1 teaspoon baking soda
½ teaspoon salt
½ teaspoon ground allspice
¼ teaspoon ground nutmeg
¾ cup butter or margarine, softened
¾ cup granulated sugar
½ cup packed light brown sugar
2 eggs
1 cup LIBBY'S® Solid Pack Pumpkin
Glaze (recipe follows)
Sliced almonds, toasted (optional)

In medium bowl, combine flour, pecans, cinnamon, baking soda, salt, allspice, and nutmeg; set aside. In large mixer bowl, cream butter and sugars. Add eggs; beat until light and fluffy. Mix in pumpkin. Add liquid ingredients to dry ingredients; mix well. Spread into greased and floured 9×5-inch loaf pan. Bake in 325°F. oven for approximately 1 hour 15 minutes, or until toothpick comes out clean. Cool in pan for 10 minutes. Remove from pan; cool on wire rack. Drizzle glaze over cake; garnish with almonds, if desired.

Glaze: In small bowl, combine 1 cup sifted powdered sugar and 3 to 4 teaspoons water.

■ Old-Fashioned Rice Pudding

Makes 10 servings

4 cups cold milk
1 cup MINUTE® Rice
1 package (4-serving size) JELL-O® Vanilla or
Coconut Cream Flavor Pudding and Pie
Filling
¼ cup raisins (optional)
1 egg, well beaten
¼ teaspoon ground cinnamon
⅛ teaspoon ground nutmeg

Combine milk, rice, pudding mix, raisins and egg in medium saucepan. Bring to a full boil over medium heat, stirring constantly. Remove from heat. Cool 5 minutes, stirring twice. Pour into individual dessert dishes or serving bowl. Sprinkle with cinnamon and nutmeg; serve warm. (For chilled pudding, place plastic wrap directly on hot pudding. Cool slightly; chill about 1 hour. Stir before serving; sprinkle with cinnamon and nutmeg.)

Old-Fashioned Fruited Rice Pudding: Add 1 can (17½ oz.) drained fruit cocktail to pudding after cooling 5 minutes. Garnish as desired.

Top: Old-Fashioned Fruited Rice Pudding;
bottom: Old-Fashioned Rice Pudding

■ Brandied Fruit Pie

Makes 8 servings

1 KEEBLER® Ready-Crust® Graham Cracker
   Pie Crust
2 packages (8 ounces each) mixed, pitted
   dried fruit
¾ cup plus 1 tablespoon water
¼ cup plus 1 tablespoon brandy or cognac
5 thin lemon slices
¾ cup packed brown sugar
1 teaspoon ground cinnamon
¼ teaspoon ground nutmeg
¼ teaspoon ground cloves
¼ teaspoon salt
½ cup graham cracker crumbs
¼ cup butter or margarine, melted
   Hard sauce or whipped cream (optional)
   Lemon slices for garnish

In medium saucepan, combine dried fruit, ¾ cup
of the water, ¼ cup of the brandy and the 5 lemon
slices. Simmer over low heat 10 minutes or until
liquid is absorbed. Remove and discard lemon
slices. Stir in sugar, spices, salt, remaining 1
tablespoon water and remaining 1 tablespoon
brandy; pour into pie crust. Sprinkle graham
cracker crumbs evenly over top of pie. Drizzle
melted butter over crumbs. Bake in preheated
350° oven 30 minutes. Cool on wire rack. Serve
warm or at room temperature. If desired, serve
with hard sauce or whipped cream; garnish with
lemon slices.

Brandied Fruit Pie

■ Chilled Chocolate Rum Souffle

Makes 6 to 8 servings

1 envelope unflavored gelatin
¼ cup cold water
4 squares BAKER'S® Unsweetened Chocolate
¼ cup dark rum*
6 eggs, separated**
⅔ cup sugar
¼ teaspoon salt
1 cup heavy cream***
2 tablespoons sugar***
½ teaspoon vanilla***

Soften gelatin in water. Melt chocolate in
saucepan over very low heat, stirring constantly
until smooth. Stir in rum and softened gelatin; stir
until gelatin is dissolved. Remove from heat.
Combine egg yolks and ⅔ cup sugar in top of
double boiler. Place over hot water and beat with
hand or electric mixer until thick and light in
color. Remove from hot water. Blend in chocolate
mixture; pour into a bowl.

Beat egg whites with salt until stiff peaks form;
fold into chocolate mixture. Whip cream with 2
tablespoons sugar and the vanilla until soft peaks
form. Fold into chocolate mixture. Pour into
buttered 1½-quart serving dish or 1-quart souffle
dish fitted with paper collar (see Note). Chill at
least 3 hours. Garnish with additional sweetened
whipped cream and chocolate curls, if desired.

Or use ¼ cup milk and 1 teaspoon rum extract.

**Use clean eggs with no cracks in shells.*

***Or use 2 cups thawed COOL WHIP® Whipped
Topping.*

Note: To make paper collar, cut a piece of waxed
paper long enough to wrap around dish and
overlap slightly. Fold in half lengthwise; grease
one side lightly with shortening. Wrap the
doubled paper around dish, greased side toward
dish, extending it 2 inches above rim. Secure with
string or tape. Remove paper collar before
serving.

Classic Christmas Cake

■ Classic Christmas Cake

Makes one 10-inch cake

   1 package (8 ounces) cream cheese, softened
   1 cup butter or margarine, softened
1½ cups granulated sugar
1½ teaspoons vanilla
1½ teaspoons ground cinnamon
   ¼ teaspoon ground nutmeg
   4 eggs
2¼ cups sifted cake flour
1½ teaspoons baking powder
   1 jar (8 ounces) maraschino cherries,
       drained and chopped
   1 cup finely chopped pecans
1½ cups powdered sugar
   2 tablespoons milk
       Pecan halves and red and green candied
       cherries for garnish

In large bowl, beat cream cheese, butter, granulated sugar, vanilla and spices. Add eggs, 1 at a time, mixing well after each addition. In small bowl, combine flour with baking powder; gradually add 2 cups of the flour mixture to butter mixture. To remaining flour mixture, add maraschino cherries and ½ cup of the chopped pecans; fold into batter. Grease 10-inch Bundt® or tube pan; sprinkle with remaining ½ cup chopped pecans. Pour batter into prepared pan. Bake in preheated 325° oven 1 hour and 15 minutes or until toothpick inserted into center of cake comes out clean. Let cool in pan on wire rack 5 minutes. Loosen edge; remove from pan. Cool completely on wire rack. In small bowl, beat powdered sugar and milk until smooth. Spoon icing over cake. Garnish with pecan halves and candied cherries.

Favorite Recipe from **National Pecan Marketing Council, Inc.**

■ Apple Streusel Mince Pie

Makes one 9-inch pie

3 all-purpose apples, pared and thinly sliced
½ cup plus 3 tablespoons unsifted flour
2 tablespoons margarine or butter, melted
1 (9-inch) unbaked pastry shell
1 jar NONE SUCH® Ready-to-Use Mincemeat
    (Regular *or* Brandy & Rum)
¼ cup firmly packed light brown sugar
1 teaspoon ground cinnamon
⅓ cup cold margarine or butter
¼ cup chopped nuts

In large bowl, toss apples with *3 tablespoons* flour and melted margarine; arrange in pastry shell. Top with mincemeat. In medium bowl, combine remaining *½ cup* flour, sugar and cinnamon; cut in cold margarine until crumbly. Add nuts; sprinkle over mincemeat. Bake in lower half of 425° oven 10 minutes. Reduce oven temperature to 375°; bake 25 minutes longer or until golden. Cool. Garnish as desired.

■ Old-Fashioned Bread Pudding

Makes about 4 cups or 6 servings

1 package (4-serving size) JELL-O® Vanilla
    Flavor Pudding and Pie Filling
¼ cup sugar
3 cups milk
¼ cup raisins
2 tablespoons grated lemon rind (optional)
1 tablespoon butter or margarine
½ teaspoon vanilla
6 slices dry white bread, cut into cubes
¼ teaspoon cinnamon
⅛ teaspoon nutmeg

Combine pudding mix and 2 tablespoons of the sugar in medium saucepan. Add 2 cups of the milk; blend well. Add raisins and lemon rind. Cook and stir over medium heat until mixture comes to a full boil. Remove from heat; stir in butter and vanilla.

Pour remaining milk over bread cubes in bowl to moisten; stir into pudding mixture. Pour into 1-quart baking dish. Combine remaining sugar with spices. Sprinkle over pudding. Broil until sugar is lightly browned and bubbly, 4 to 5 minutes. Serve warm or chilled. Garnish with lemon slice, if desired.

Apple Streusel Mince Pie

■ Eggnog Pie

Makes one 9-inch pie

> 1 cup cold dairy or canned eggnog
> 1 package (6-serving size) JELL-O® Vanilla Flavor Instant Pudding and Pie Filling
> 1 tablespoon rum or ¼ teaspoon rum extract
> ¼ teaspoon nutmeg
> 3½ cups (8 ounces) COOL WHIP® Non-Dairy Whipped Topping, thawed
> 1 prepared 8- to 9-inch graham cracker crumb crust, cooled

Pour cold eggnog into bowl. Add pie filling mix, rum and nutmeg. With electric mixer at low speed, beat until blended, about 1 minute. Let stand 5 minutes. Fold in 2 cups of the whipped topping. Spoon into pie crust. Chill until firm, about 2 hours. Garnish with remaining whipped topping. Sprinkle with additional nutmeg, if desired.

■ Linzer Bars

Makes 2 dozen small bars

> ¾ cup butter or margarine, softened
> ½ cup sugar
> 1 egg
> ½ teaspoon grated lemon peel
> ¼ teaspoon salt
> ½ teaspoon ground cinnamon
> ⅛ teaspoon ground cloves
> 2 cups all-purpose flour
> 1 cup DIAMOND® Walnuts, finely chopped or ground
> 1 cup raspberry or apricot jam

In large bowl, cream butter, sugar, egg, lemon peel, salt and spices. Blend in flour and walnuts. Set aside about ¼ of the dough for lattice top. Pat remaining dough into bottom and about ½ inch up sides of greased 9-inch square pan. Spread with jam. Make pencil-shaped strips of remaining dough, rolling against floured board with palms of hands. Arrange in lattice pattern over top, pressing ends against dough on sides. Bake in preheated 325°F oven about 45 minutes or until lightly browned. Cool in pan, then cut into bars.

Cherry-Topped Icebox Cake

■ Cherry-Topped Icebox Cake

Makes 12 servings

> 20 whole graham crackers
> 2 cups cold milk
> 1 package (6-serving size) JELL-O® Vanilla or Chocolate Flavor Instant Pudding and Pie Filling
> 1¾ cups thawed COOL WHIP® Non-Dairy Whipped Topping
> 2 cans (21 ounces each) cherry pie filling

Line 13×9-inch pan with some of the graham crackers, breaking crackers, if necessary. Pour cold milk into bowl. Add pudding mix. With electric mixer at low speed, beat until well blended, 1 to 2 minutes. Let stand 5 minutes; then blend in whipped topping. Spread half of the pudding mixture over crackers. Add another layer of crackers. Top with remaining pudding mixture and remaining crackers. Spread cherry pie filling over crackers. Chill about 3 hours.

Chocolate-Frosted Icebox Cake: Prepare Cherry-Topped Icebox Cake as directed, substituting ¾ cup ready-to-spread chocolate fudge frosting for the cherry pie filling. Carefully spread frosting over top layer of graham crackers.

■ Scrumptious Chocolate Layer Bars

About 3 dozen bars

> 2 cups (12-ounce package) HERSHEY'S Semi-Sweet Chocolate Chips
> 1 package (8 ounces) cream cheese
> ½ cup plus 2 tablespoons (5-ounce can) evaporated milk
> 1 cup chopped walnuts
> ¼ cup sesame seeds (optional)
> ½ teaspoon almond extract
> 3 cups all-purpose flour
> 1½ cups sugar
> 1 teaspoon baking powder
> ½ teaspoon salt
> 1 cup butter or margarine
> 2 eggs
> ½ teaspoon almond extract

Combine chocolate chips, cream cheese and evaporated milk in medium saucepan. Cook over low heat, stirring constantly, until chips are melted and mixture is smooth. Remove from heat; stir in walnuts, sesame seeds and ½ teaspoon almond extract. Blend well; set aside.

Combine remaining ingredients in large mixer bowl; blend well on low speed until mixture resembles coarse crumbs. Press half the crumb mixture in greased 13×9-inch pan; spread with chocolate mixture. Sprinkle rest of crumb mixture over filling. (If crumb mixture softens and forms a stiff dough, pinch off small pieces to use as topping.) Bake at 375°for 35 to 40 minutes or until golden brown. Cool; cut into bars.

■ Peanut Butter Paisley Brownies

About 3 dozen brownies

> ½ cup butter or margarine, softened
> ¼ cup peanut butter
> 1 cup granulated sugar
> 1 cup packed light brown sugar
> 3 eggs
> 1 teaspoon vanilla extract
> 2 cups all-purpose flour
> 2 teaspoons baking powder
> ¼ teaspoon salt
> ½ cup (5.5-ounce can) HERSHEY'S Syrup

Blend butter and peanut butter in large mixer bowl. Add granulated sugar and brown sugar; beat well. Add eggs, one at a time, beating well after each addition. Blend in vanilla. Combine flour, baking powder and salt; add to peanut butter mixture.

Spread half the batter in greased 13×9-inch pan. Spoon syrup over top. Carefully spread with remaining batter. Swirl with spatula or knife for marbled effect. Bake at 350° for 35 to 40 minutes or until lightly browned. Cool; cut into squares.

■ Best Brownies

About 16 brownies

> ½ cup butter or margarine, melted
> 1 cup sugar
> 1 teaspoon vanilla extract
> 2 eggs
> ½ cup all-purpose flour
> ⅓ cup HERSHEY'S Cocoa
> ¼ teaspoon baking powder
> ¼ teaspoon salt
> ½ cup chopped nuts (optional)
> Creamy Brownie Frosting (recipe follows)

Blend butter, sugar and vanilla in large bowl. Add eggs; using a wooden spoon, beat well. Combine flour, cocoa, baking powder and salt; gradually blend into egg mixture. Stir in nuts.

Spread in greased 9-inch square pan. Bake at 350° for 20 to 25 minutes or until brownie begins to pull away from edges of pan. Cool; frost with Creamy Brownie Frosting. Cut into squares.

Creamy Brownie Frosting

About 1 cup frosting

> 3 tablespoons butter or margarine, softened
> 3 tablespoons HERSHEY'S Cocoa
> 1 tablespoon light corn syrup or honey
> ½ teaspoon vanilla extract
> 1 cup confectioners' sugar
> 1 to 2 tablespoons milk

Cream butter, cocoa, corn syrup and vanilla in small mixer bowl. Add confectioners' sugar and milk; beat to spreading consistency.

Clockwise from top left: Peanut Butter Paisley Brownies, Scrumptious Chocolate Layer Bars and Best Brownies

Rosettes

■ Rosettes

Makes 3 dozen rosettes

CRISCO® Oil for frying
1 cup unsifted all-purpose flour
2 tablespoons confectioners sugar
¼ teaspoon salt
1 cup milk
2 eggs
1 teaspoon vanilla
1 teaspoon almond extract
Confectioners sugar

Heat 2 to 3 inches CRISCO Oil in deep-fryer or large saucepan to 365°F. Meanwhile, mix flour, 2 tablespoons confectioners sugar and salt in small mixing bowl. Add milk, eggs, vanilla and almond extract. Stir until smooth.

Place rosette iron in hot CRISCO Oil 1 minute. Tap excess oil from iron onto paper towel. Dip hot iron into batter, making sure batter does not cover top of iron. Place back into hot oil. Fry about 30 seconds, or until rosette is golden brown. Immediately remove rosette. Drain on paper towels. Reheat iron in hot oil 1 minute before frying each rosette. Sprinkle rosettes with confectioners sugar.

■ Cherry Cheese Pie

Makes one 9-inch pie

1 (9-inch) graham cracker crumb crust *or* baked pastry shell
1 (8-ounce) package cream cheese, softened
1 (14-ounce) can EAGLE® Brand Sweetened Condensed Milk (NOT evaporated milk)
⅓ cup REALEMON® Lemon Juice from Concentrate
1 teaspoon vanilla extract
1 (21-ounce) can cherry pie filling, chilled

In large bowl, beat cheese until fluffy. Gradually beat in sweetened condensed milk until smooth. Stir in ReaLemon® brand and vanilla. Pour into prepared crust. Chill 3 hours or until set. Top with desired amount of pie filling before serving. Refrigerate leftovers.

TOPPING VARIATIONS

Fresh Fruit: Omit cherry pie filling. Arrange well-drained fresh strawberries, banana slices (dipped in ReaLemon® brand and well-drained) and blueberries on top of chilled pie. Just before serving, brush fruit with light corn syrup if desired.

Ambrosia: Omit cherry pie filling. In small saucepan, combine ½ cup peach *or* apricot preserves, ¼ cup flaked coconut, 2 tablespoons orange juice *or* orange-flavored liqueur and 2 teaspoons cornstarch; cook and stir until thickened. Remove from heat. Arrange fresh orange sections over top of pie; top with coconut mixture. Chill.

Blueberry: Omit cherry pie filling. In medium saucepan, combine ¼ cup sugar and 1 tablespoon cornstarch; mix well. Add ½ cup water, 2 tablespoons ReaLemon® brand then 2 cups fresh or dry-pack frozen blueberries; mix well. Bring to a boil; reduce heat and simmer 3 minutes or until thickened and clear. Cool 10 minutes. Spread over pie. Chill.

Cranberry: Omit cherry pie filling. In medium saucepan, combine ⅓ cup sugar and 1 tablespoon cornstarch. Add ½ cup plus 2 tablespoons cold water and 2 cups fresh or dry-pack frozen cranberries; mix well. Bring to a boil; reduce heat and simmer 10 minutes, stirring constantly. Cool 15 minutes. Spread over pie. Chill.

Banana Cream Cheese Pie: Omit cherry pie filling. Prepare filling as above. Slice 2 bananas; dip in ReaLemon® brand and drain. Line crust with bananas. Pour filling over bananas; cover. Chill. Before serving, slice 2 bananas; dip in ReaLemon® brand and drain. Garnish top of pie with bananas.

■ Colonial Apple Cake

1 ring cake

2¾ cups unsifted all-purpose flour
  1 teaspoon baking powder
  1 teaspoon ground cinnamon
  ¾ teaspoon salt
  ½ teaspoon baking soda
1¾ cups granulated sugar
1¼ cups CRISCO® Oil
  2 eggs
  ¼ cup milk
  1 teaspoon vanilla
  2 cups chopped, peeled apple
  ½ cup chopped dates
  1 teaspoon grated lemon peel
  1 to 2 tablespoons confectioners sugar

Preheat oven to 350°F. Grease and flour 12-cup fluted ring pan. Set aside.

Mix flour, baking powder, cinnamon, salt and baking soda in medium mixing bowl. Set aside. Combine granulated sugar, CRISCO Oil, eggs, milk and vanilla in large mixing bowl. Beat with electric mixer at medium speed until blended, scraping bowl constantly. Add dry ingredients. Beat at medium speed 2 minutes longer, scraping bowl frequently. Stir in apple, dates and lemon peel. Pour into prepared pan.

Bake at 350°F, 1 hour to 1 hour 15 minutes, or until wooden pick inserted in center comes out clean. Let stand 10 minutes. Invert onto serving plate. Cool slightly. Sift confectioners sugar onto cake. Serve warm. Top with *whipped cream*, if desired.

Colonial Apple Cake

■ Swirl of Chocolate Cheesecake Squares

Makes sixteen, 2-inch squares

CRUST
- 1 cup graham cracker crumbs
- ¼ cup butter or margarine, melted
- 3 tablespoons sugar

FILLING
- 1 package (8 ounces) cream cheese, softened
- ¾ cup *undiluted* CARNATION® Evaporated Milk
- ½ cup sugar
- 1 egg, lightly beaten
- 2 tablespoons all-purpose flour
- 2 teaspoons vanilla extract
- ½ cup (3 ounces) semi-sweet chocolate chips or pieces, melted

For Crust: In small bowl, combine crumbs, butter, and sugar. Firmly press mixture into bottom of buttered 8×8-inch baking pan.

For Filling: In blender container, place cream cheese, evaporated milk, sugar, egg, flour, and vanilla; process until smooth. Gradually stir ½ *cup* cheese mixture into melted chocolate. Pour *remaining* cheese mixture into crust. Pour chocolate mixture over cheese mixture. Swirl mixtures together with knife or spoon to create marbled effect. Bake in preheated 300°F. oven for 40 to 45 minutes, or until set. Cool in pan on wire rack before cutting. Store, covered, in refrigerator.

■ Simply Superb Pecan Pie

Makes one 9-inch pie

- 3 eggs, beaten
- 1 cup sugar
- ½ cup dark corn syrup
- 1 teaspoon vanilla
- 6 tablespoons butter or margarine, melted, cooled
- 1 cup pecan pieces or halves
- 1 (9-inch) unbaked pie shell

In large bowl, beat eggs, sugar, corn syrup, vanilla and butter. Stir in pecans. Pour into unbaked pie shell. Bake in preheated 350° oven 45 to 60 minutes or until knife inserted halfway between outside and center comes out clean. Cool on wire rack.

Favorite Recipe from **National Pecan Marketing Council, Inc.**

Simply Superb Pecan Pie

■ Sweet Potato Custard Pie

Makes one 9-inch pie

    Pecan Crust (recipe follows)*
3 eggs
1 can (16 ounces) vacuum-packed sweet
    potatoes, drained, mashed
½ cup packed brown sugar
1½ teaspoons ground cinnamon
1 teaspoon ground allspice
½ teaspoon salt
1 can (13 ounces) evaporated milk
    Whipped cream (optional)
    Pecan halves (optional)

Prepare Pecan Crust. In large bowl, beat eggs, sweet potatoes, sugar, spices and salt. In small saucepan, heat evaporated milk over medium heat until hot; gradually stir into sweet potato mixture. Pour into unbaked pie shell. Bake in lower third of preheated 400° oven 40 to 45 minutes or until knife inserted near center comes out clean. Cool completely on wire rack. If desired, garnish with whipped cream and pecan halves.

A thawed frozen 9-inch deep-dish-style pie shell may be substituted.

Pecan Crust

1½ cups all-purpose flour
¼ cup ground pecans
½ teaspoon salt
½ cup shortening
1 egg yolk
4 to 5 tablespoons ice water
2 teaspoons lemon juice

In large bowl, combine flour, ground pecans and salt. Cut in shortening until mixture resembles coarse crumbs. In small bowl, blend egg yolk, 4 tablespoons of the water and the lemon juice. Add to flour mixture, mixing lightly with fork until dough just sticks together. Add more water, if necessary. Press into ball. Roll out on lightly floured surface into 10-inch circle. Carefully fit into 9-inch pie plate. Trim edge; flute as desired. Prick bottom and side of pastry with fork.

Favorite Recipe from American Egg Board

Applesauce Fruitcake Bars

■ Applesauce Fruitcake Bars

Makes 48 bars

1 (14-ounce) can EAGLE® Brand Sweetened
    Condensed Milk (NOT evaporated milk)
2 eggs
¼ cup margarine or butter, melted
2 teaspoons vanilla extract
3 cups biscuit baking mix
1 (15-ounce) jar applesauce
1 cup chopped dates
1 (6-ounce) container green candied
    cherries, chopped
1 (6-ounce) container red candied cherries,
    chopped
1 cup chopped nuts
1 cup raisins
    Confectioners' sugar

Preheat oven to 325°. In large mixer bowl, beat sweetened condensed milk, eggs, margarine and vanilla. Stir in remaining ingredients except confectioners' sugar. Spread evenly into well-greased and floured 15×10-inch jellyroll pan. Bake 35 to 40 minutes or until wooden pick inserted in center comes out clean. Cool thoroughly. Sprinkle with confectioners' sugar. Cut into bars. Store tightly covered at room temperature.

■ Christmas Tree Cake

Makes 12 to 16 servings

1 two-layer cake mix (any flavor)
Ingredients for cake mix
Decorator Frosting (recipe follows)
Assorted decorative candies

Preheat oven to 350°F. Prepare batter as directed on box. Pour into well-greased and floured Christmas tree cake pan. Bake 45 to 55 minutes or until wooden pick inserted in cake in widest part of pan comes out clean. Cool cake in pan 10 minutes on wire rack. Carefully run straight-edged knife or spatula around edge of cake to loosen; gently remove cake from pan. Cool cake completely. Meanwhile, prepare Decorator Frosting. Carefully transfer cake to large serving tray or board. Spread with frosting. Decorate with candies as desired to resemble decorated Christmas tree.

Decorator Frosting

Makes about 1½ cups

3 cups sifted powdered sugar
⅓ cup shortening
3 tablespoons water
1 tablespoon light corn syrup
½ teaspoon vanilla
Green food coloring

Combine ingredients in large bowl of electric mixer. Beat at medium speed until well blended. Beat at high speed 5 minutes. Tint with food coloring to desired color.

■ Pumpkin Trifle

Makes 12 servings

1 pound cake (16 ounces), cut into 12 slices
6 tablespoons orange juice
1 cup (14-ounce jar) cranberry-orange relish
3 cups whipping cream
¾ cup sifted powdered sugar
2 cups LIBBY'S Pumpkin Pie Mix
1 cup sliced almonds, toasted

Drizzle cake slices with orange juice. Spread with relish; set aside. In large bowl, beat whipping cream and powdered sugar until stiff peaks form; fold in pumpkin pie mix.

To Assemble: In trifle bowl, arrange 4 cake slices on bottom. Layer with 3 cups pumpkin mixture, and ⅓ cup almonds; repeat layers two more times. Cover; chill several hours or overnight. Garnish as desired.

Note: Sherry or orange liqueur may be substituted for orange juice.

■ Easy Carrot Cake

Makes 10 to 12 servings

1 two-layer yellow cake mix
1¼ cups MIRACLE WHIP Salad Dressing
4 eggs
¼ cup cold water
2 teaspoons ground cinnamon
2 cups finely shredded carrots
½ cup chopped walnuts
Vanilla "Philly" Frosting (recipe follows)

In large bowl of electric mixer, combine cake mix, salad dressing, eggs, water and cinnamon, mixing at medium speed until well blended. Stir in carrots and walnuts. Pour into greased 13×9-inch baking pan. Bake at 350°, 35 minutes or until wooden pick inserted in center comes out clean. Cool. Frost with Vanilla "Philly" Frosting.

Preparation time: 25 minutes

Baking time: 35 minutes plus cooling

Vanilla "Philly" Frosting

1 3-oz. pkg. PHILADELPHIA BRAND Cream Cheese, softened
1 tablespoon milk
½ teaspoon vanilla
3 cups sifted powdered sugar

Combine cream cheese, milk and vanilla, mixing until well blended. Gradually add sugar, beating until light and fluffy.

Marble Cheesecake

■ Marble Cheesecake

10 to 12 servings

    Graham Crust (recipe follows)
  **3 packages (8 ounces each) cream cheese,
    softened**
  ¾ cup sugar
  ½ cup dairy sour cream
  2 teaspoons vanilla extract
  3 tablespoons all-purpose flour
  3 eggs
  ¼ cup HERSHEY'S Cocoa
  ¼ cup sugar
  1 tablespoon vegetable oil
  ½ teaspoon vanilla extract

Prepare Graham Crust; set aside. Combine cream cheese, ¾ cup sugar, the sour cream and 2 teaspoons vanilla in large mixer bowl; beat on medium speed until smooth. Add flour, 1 tablespoon at a time, blending well. Add eggs; beat well. Combine cocoa and ¼ cup sugar in small bowl. Add oil, ½ teaspoon vanilla and 1½ cups of the cream cheese mixture; mix until well blended.

Spoon plain and chocolate mixtures alternately into prepared crust, ending with dollops of chocolate on top; gently swirl with knife or spatula for marbled effect. Bake at 450° for 10 minutes; without opening oven door, decrease temperature to 250° and continue to bake for 30 minutes. Turn off oven; let cheesecake remain in oven 30 minutes without opening door. Remove from oven; loosen cake from side of pan. Cool completely; chill thoroughly.

Graham Crust

  1 cup graham cracker crumbs
  2 tablespoons sugar
  ¼ cup butter or margarine, melted

Combine graham cracker crumbs, sugar and melted butter. Press mixture onto bottom and ½ inch up side of 9-inch springform pan. Bake at 350° for 8 to 10 minutes; cool.

Cookies & Candies

■ Cream Cheese Cutout Cookies

Makes about 90 cookies

1 cup butter, softened
1 8-ounce package cream cheese, softened
1½ cups sugar
1 egg
1 teaspoon vanilla
½ teaspoon almond extract
3½ cups all-purpose flour
1 teaspoon baking powder
Almond Frosting (recipe follows)

In a large mixer bowl combine butter and cream cheese. Beat until well combined. Add sugar; beat until fluffy. Add egg, vanilla, and almond extract and beat well.

In a medium bowl stir together flour and baking powder. Add flour mixture to cream cheese mixture; beat until well mixed. Divide dough in half. Cover and chill in the refrigerator about 1½ hours or until dough is easy to handle.

On a lightly floured surface roll dough to ⅛-inch thickness. Cut with desired cookie cutters. Place on an ungreased cookie sheet. Bake in a 375° oven for 8 to 10 minutes or until done. Remove to wire racks; cool. Pipe or spread Almond Frosting onto cooled cookies.

Almond Frosting: In a small mixer bowl beat 2 cups sifted *powdered sugar,* 2 tablespoons softened *butter,* and ¼ teaspoon *almond extract* until smooth. Beat in enough *milk* (4 to 5 teaspoons) until of piping consistency. For spreadable icing, add a little more milk. Stir in a few drops of *food coloring,* if desired. Garnish with colored sugar, dragées or nuts, if desired.

Favorite Recipe from **Wisconsin Milk Marketing Board** © 1989

■ Dutch St. Nicolas Cookies

Makes about 3½ dozen cookies

½ cup whole natural almonds
¾ cup butter or margarine, softened
½ cup packed brown sugar
2 tablespoons milk
1½ teaspoons ground cinnamon
¼ teaspoon ground nutmeg
¼ teaspoon ground ginger
¼ teaspoon ground cloves
2 cups sifted all-purpose flour
1½ teaspoons baking powder
½ teaspoon salt
¼ cup coarsely chopped citron

Spread almonds in single layer on baking sheet. Bake at 375°F, 10 to 12 minutes, stirring occasionally, until lightly toasted. Cool. Chop finely. In large bowl, cream butter, sugar, milk and spices. In small bowl, combine flour, baking powder and salt. Add flour mixture to creamed mixture; blend well. Stir in almonds and citron. Knead dough slightly to make ball. Cover; refrigerate until firm. Roll out dough ¼ inch thick on lightly floured surface. Cut out with cookie cutters. Place 2 inches apart on greased cookie sheets. Bake at 375°F, 7 to 10 minutes, until lightly browned. Remove to wire racks to cool.

Favorite Recipe from **Almond Board of California**

Cream Cheese Cutout Cookies

■ Rich Cocoa Fudge

About 3 dozen candies

   3 cups sugar
   ⅔ cup HERSHEY'S Cocoa
   ⅛ teaspoon salt
1½ cups milk
   ¼ cup butter or margarine
   1 teaspoon vanilla extract

Butter 8- or 9-inch square pan; set aside. Combine sugar, cocoa and salt in heavy 4-quart saucepan; stir in milk. Cook over medium heat, stirring constantly, until mixture comes to full rolling boil. Boil, without stirring, to soft-ball stage, 234°F on a candy thermometer (or until syrup, when dropped into very cold water, forms a soft ball that flattens when removed from water). Bulb of candy thermometer should not rest on bottom of saucepan.

Remove from heat. Add butter and vanilla; *do not stir.* Cool at room temperature to 110°F (lukewarm). Beat until fudge thickens and loses some of its gloss. Quickly spread in prepared pan; cool. Cut into 1- to 1½-inch squares.

VARIATIONS

Nutty Rich Cocoa Fudge: Beat cooked fudge as directed. *Immediately* stir in 1 cup broken almonds, pecans or walnuts and quickly spread in prepared pan.

Marshmallow-Nut Cocoa Fudge: Increase cocoa to ¾ cup. Cook fudge as directed. Add 1 cup marshmallow creme with butter and vanilla; *do not stir.* Cool to 110°F. (lukewarm). Beat 10 minutes; stir in 1 cup broken nuts and pour into prepared pan. (Fudge does not set until poured into pan.)

Top to bottom: Double-Decker Fudge, Chocolate-Almond Fudge and Nutty Rich Cocoa Fudge

■ Chocolate-Almond Fudge

About 5 dozen

4 cups sugar
1¾ cups (7-ounce jar) marshmallow creme
1½ cups (12-ounce can) evaporated milk
1 tablespoon butter or margarine
2 cups (12-ounce package) HERSHEY'S MINI
    CHIPS Semi-Sweet Chocolate
1 HERSHEY'S Milk Chocolate Bar with
    Almonds (8 ounces), chopped
1 teaspoon vanilla extract
¾ cup chopped slivered almonds

Butter 9-inch square pan; set aside. Combine sugar, marshmallow creme, evaporated milk and butter in heavy 4-quart saucepan. Cook over medium heat, stirring constantly, until mixture comes to a full boil; boil and stir 7 minutes. Remove from heat; *immediately* add MINI CHIPS Chocolate and chocolate bar pieces, stirring until completely melted. Blend in vanilla; stir in almonds. Pour into prepared pan; cool completely. Cut into 1-inch squares.

Chocolate Pixies

■ Double-Decker Fudge

About 4 dozen candies

1 cup REESE'S Peanut Butter Chips
1 cup HERSHEY'S Semi-Sweet Chocolate
    Chips
2¼ cups sugar
1¾ cups (7-ounce jar) marshmallow creme
¾ cup evaporated milk
¼ cup butter or margarine
1 teaspoon vanilla extract

Measure peanut butter chips into one bowl and chocolate chips into another; set aside. Butter 8-inch square pan; set aside. Combine sugar, marshmallow creme, evaporated milk and butter in heavy 3-quart saucepan. Cook over medium heat, stirring constantly, until mixture boils; continue cooking and stirring for 5 minutes.

Remove from heat; stir in vanilla. Immediately stir half the hot mixture into peanut butter chips until completely melted. Quickly pour into prepared pan. Stir remaining hot mixture into chocolate chips until completely melted. Quickly spread over top of peanut butter layer; cool. Cut into 1-inch squares.

■ Chocolate Pixies

Makes 4 dozen cookies

¼ cup LAND O LAKES® Sweet Cream Butter
4 squares (1 ounce each) unsweetened
    chocolate
2 cups all-purpose flour
2 cups granulated sugar
4 eggs
2 teaspoons baking powder
½ teaspoon salt
½ cup chopped walnuts or pecans
    Powdered sugar

In small saucepan over low heat, melt butter and chocolate; stir to blend. Cool. In large bowl, beat chocolate mixture, 1 cup of the flour, the granulated sugar, eggs, baking powder and salt until well mixed. Stir in remaining 1 cup flour and the nuts. Cover; refrigerate until firm, 2 hours or overnight. Shape teaspoonfuls of dough into 1-inch balls; roll in powdered sugar. Place 2 inches apart on greased cookie sheets. Bake in preheated 300° oven 12 to 15 minutes or until firm to the touch. Remove to wire racks to cool.

Crisp Peanut Butter Cookies

Makes 6 dozen cookies

2½ cups all-purpose flour
 1 teaspoon baking powder
 1 teaspoon baking soda
 ¼ teaspoon salt
 1 cup MAZOLA® Margarine, softened
 1 cup SKIPPY® Creamy or SUPER CHUNK™
   Peanut Butter
 1 cup granulated sugar
 1 cup packed brown sugar
 2 eggs
 1 teaspoon vanilla
   Granulated sugar

In small bowl, combine flour, baking powder, baking soda and salt. In large bowl, beat margarine and peanut butter until well blended. Beat in sugars until blended. Beat in eggs and vanilla. Add flour mixture; beat until well blended. If dough is too soft to handle, cover and refrigerate until firm. Shape dough into 1-inch balls. Place 2 inches apart on ungreased cookie sheets. Using back of fork dipped in granulated sugar, flatten balls making crisscross pattern. Bake in preheated 350° oven 12 minutes or until lightly browned. Remove to wire racks to cool completely.

Cherry-Coconut Peanut Butter Cookies: Prepare cookie dough as directed; shape into 1-inch balls. Roll balls in 2 cans (3½ ounces each) flaked coconut. *Do not flatten.* Place red or green candied cherry half in center of each cookie. Bake as directed for 15 minutes. Makes 6 dozen cookies.

Cloverleaf Cookies: Prepare cookie dough as directed; divide into 3 parts. Stir ⅓ cup miniature semisweet chocolate chips into first part. Stir ⅔ cup miniature semisweet chocolate chips, melted, into second part. Leave third part plain. To form each cookie, shape ½ teaspoon of each dough into a ball. Place balls cloverleaf-style on ungreased cookie sheets, leaving 2 inches between clusters. Bake as directed. Let cookies cool 1 minute before carefully removing from cookie sheets to wire racks. Makes 5 dozen cookies.

Counterclockwise from top left: Peanut Butter Cutouts (page 74), Cherry-Coconut Peanut Butter Cookies, Peanut Butter Crackles, Santa Lollipop Cookies (page 74), Crisp Peanut Butter Cookies, Peanut Butter Gingerbread Men (page 74) and Peanut Butter Chocolate Chip Cookies

Peanut Butter Crackles

Makes about 5 dozen cookies

1½ cups all-purpose flour
 1 teaspoon baking soda
 ⅛ teaspoon salt
 ½ cup MAZOLA® Margarine, softened
 ½ cup SKIPPY® Creamy or SUPER CHUNK™
   Peanut Butter
 ½ cup granulated sugar
 ½ cup packed brown sugar
 1 egg
 1 teaspoon vanilla
   Granulated sugar
   Chocolate candy stars

In small bowl, combine flour, baking soda and salt. In large bowl, beat margarine and peanut butter until well blended. Beat in sugars until blended. Beat in egg and vanilla. Gradually beat in flour mixture until well mixed. Shape dough into 1-inch balls. Roll in granulated sugar. Place 2 inches apart on ungreased cookie sheets. Bake in preheated 375° oven 10 minutes or until lightly browned. Remove from oven and quickly press chocolate star firmly into top of each cookie (cookie will crack around edges). Remove to wire racks to cool completely.

Peanut Butter Chocolate Chip Cookies

Makes about 3½ dozen cookies

 1 cup sugar
 ½ cup SKIPPY® Creamy or SUPER CHUNK™
   Peanut Butter
 ½ cup *undiluted* evaporated milk
 1 package (6 ounces) semisweet chocolate
   chips
 1 cup coarsely chopped nuts

In medium bowl, mix sugar and peanut butter until well blended. Stir in evaporated milk, chips and nuts until well mixed. Drop batter by heaping teaspoonfuls 1½ inches apart onto foil-lined cookie sheets. Spread batter evenly into 2-inch rounds. Bake in preheated 325° oven 18 to 20 minutes or until golden. Cool completely on foil on wire racks. Peel foil from cookies.

■ Peanut Butter Cutouts

Makes about 4 dozen cookies

1½ cups all-purpose flour
 ¾ teaspoon baking soda
 ⅛ teaspoon salt
 ½ cup MAZOLA® Margarine, softened
 ½ cup SKIPPY® Creamy Peanut Butter
 ½ cup granulated sugar
 ½ cup packed brown sugar
 1 egg
    Colored sugars (optional)

In small bowl, combine flour, baking soda and salt. In large bowl, beat margarine and peanut butter until well blended. Beat in granulated and brown sugars until blended. Beat in egg. Gradually beat in flour mixture until well mixed. Divide dough into thirds. Wrap each portion; refrigerate until firm, about 3 hours. Roll out dough, one third at a time, ¼ inch thick on lightly floured surface. Cut out with cookie cutters. Place 2 inches apart on ungreased cookie sheets. If desired, sprinkle cookies with colored sugars. Bake in preheated 350° oven 8 to 10 minutes or until lightly browned. Remove to wire racks to cool.

Santa Lollipop Cookies: Prepare cookie dough as above. Place lollipop sticks 3 inches apart on ungreased cookie sheets. Roll out dough ⅛ inch thick. Cut out with 4-inch Santa cookie cutter; place over 1 end of each lollipop stick. Bake as above. Decorate as desired. Makes 3 dozen cookies.

■ Peanut Butter Gingerbread Men

Makes about 2½ dozen cookies

 5 cups all-purpose flour
1½ teaspoons ground cinnamon
 1 teaspoon baking soda
 ½ teaspoon ground ginger
 ¼ teaspoon salt
 ¾ cup MAZOLA® Margarine, softened
 ¾ cup SKIPPY® Creamy Peanut Butter
 1 cup packed brown sugar
 1 cup KARO® Dark Corn Syrup
 2 eggs
    Frosting for decorating (optional)

In large bowl, combine flour, cinnamon, baking soda, ginger and salt. In another large bowl, beat margarine and peanut butter until well blended. Add sugar, corn syrup and eggs; beat until smooth. Gradually beat in 2 cups of the dry ingredients. With wooden spoon, beat in remaining dry ingredients, 1 cup at a time, until well blended. Divide dough into thirds. Wrap each portion; refrigerate until firm, at least 1 hour. Roll out dough, one third at a time, ⅛ inch thick on lightly floured surface. Cut out with 5½-inch gingerbread cutter. Place 2 inches apart on ungreased cookie sheets. Bake in preheated 300° oven 10 to 12 minutes or until very lightly browned. Remove to wire racks to cool completely. If desired, pipe frosting on cookies to make eyes and buttons.

■ Lemony Spritz Sticks

Makes about 8½ dozen

 1 cup butter or margarine, softened
 1 cup confectioners' sugar
 ¼ cup REALEMON® Lemon Juice from
    Concentrate
2½ cups unsifted flour
 ¼ teaspoon salt
    Chocolate Glaze (recipe follows)
    Finely chopped nuts

Preheat oven to 375°. In large mixer bowl, beat butter and sugar until fluffy. Add ReaLemon® brand; beat well. Stir in flour and salt; mix well. Place dough in cookie press with star-shaped plate. Press dough onto greased baking sheets into 3-inch strips. Bake 5 to 6 minutes or until lightly browned on ends. Cool 1 to 2 minutes; remove from baking sheets. Cool completely. Dip ends of cookies in Chocolate Glaze then into nuts.

Chocolate Glaze: In small saucepan, melt 3 ounces sweet cooking chocolate and 2 tablespoons margarine or butter. Makes about ⅓ cup.

Tip: When using electric cookie gun, use decorator tip. Press dough onto greased baking sheets into ½×3-inch strips. Bake 8 to 10 minutes or until lightly browned on ends.

Chocolate-Dipped Morsels

■ Chocolate-Dipped Morsels

Makes 1 to 1½ dozen

**4 squares BAKER'S® Semi-Sweet Chocolate
  Assorted morsel centers**

Melt chocolate in saucepan over very low heat,
stirring constantly until smooth. Insert wooden
picks or skewers into fruit and marshmallow
centers. Dip quickly, one at a time, into
chocolate. (To dip pretzels or nuts, stir into
chocolate; remove with fork.) Let stand or chill on
rack or waxed paper until chocolate is firm. For
best eating quality, chill dipped fresh or canned
fruits and serve the same day.

SUGGESTED MORSEL CENTERS

Fruits: Firm strawberries, ½-inch banana slices,
fresh pineapple wedges or drained canned
pineapple chunks, peeled orange slices, orange
wedges, well-drained stemmed maraschino
cherries, dried figs, dried dates or dried apricots.

Unsalted Pretzels and Large Marshmallows

Nuts: Walnut or pecan halves or whole almonds or
Brazil nuts.

■ Fruit-Filled Thumbprints

Makes 3 dozen cookies

**2 cups all-purpose flour
1 cup LAND O LAKES® Sweet Cream Butter,
  softened
½ cup packed brown sugar
2 eggs, separated
1 teaspoon vanilla
⅛ teaspoon salt
1½ cups finely chopped pecans
  Fruit preserves**

In large bowl, combine flour, butter, sugar, egg
yolks, vanilla and salt; beat until well mixed.
Shape teaspoonfuls of dough into 1-inch balls. In
small bowl, beat egg whites with fork until foamy.
Dip each ball into egg whites; roll in chopped
pecans. Place 1 inch apart on greased cookie
sheets. Make a depression in center of each cookie
with back of a teaspoon. Bake in preheated 350°
oven 8 minutes; remove from oven. Fill centers
with preserves; continue baking 6 to 10 minutes
or until lightly browned. Remove to wire racks to
cool.

■ Jingle Jumbles

Makes about 2 dozen cookies

¾ cup butter or margarine, softened
1 cup packed brown sugar
¼ cup molasses
1 egg
2¼ cups all-purpose flour
2 teaspoons baking soda
1 teaspoon ground ginger
1 teaspoon ground cinnamon
½ teaspoon ground cloves
½ teaspoon salt
1¼ cups SUN-MAID® Raisins
   Granulated sugar

In large bowl, cream butter and sugar. Add molasses and egg; beat until fluffy. In medium bowl, sift flour with soda, ginger, cinnamon, cloves and salt. Stir into molasses mixture. Stir in raisins. Cover and chill about 30 minutes. Form dough into 1½-inch balls; roll in granulated sugar, coating generously. Place 2 inches apart on greased baking sheet. Bake in preheated 375°F oven 12 to 14 minutes or until edges are firm and centers are still slightly soft. Remove to wire rack to cool.

■ Swiss Cinnamon Cookies

Makes about 3 dozen (3-inch) cookies

3 egg whites
3¼ cups powdered sugar (approximately)
3 cups DIAMOND® Walnuts, finely ground
1 tablespoon ground cinnamon
   Chopped DIAMOND® Walnuts, colored
      sugars, candied cherries, dragées, for
      garnish

In medium bowl, beat egg whites until foamy. Gradually beat in 2 cups of the sugar. Beat until mixture holds soft peaks, 3 to 4 minutes; remove ¾ cup of the batter, cover and set aside. Mix the 3 cups walnuts, the cinnamon and ¾ cup more of the sugar into larger egg white-sugar portion. Working with a third of the dough at a time, roll out to ⅛-inch thickness on pastry cloth or board heavily dusted with powdered sugar. Cut into desired shapes with cookie cutters. Place on greased or parchment-lined baking sheets. With tip of knife, spread reserved egg white mixture ⅛

Swiss Cinnamon Cookies (top, center right, bottom right), Jingle Jumbles (center left) and Festive Cookie Bars (bottom left)

inch thick onto top of each cookie, spreading almost to edges. Decorate immediately, as desired, with chopped walnuts, colored sugars, candied cherries and dragées. Bake in preheated 300°F oven 12 to 14 minutes or until cookies are just set and very lightly browned. Remove to wire racks to cool completely. Store in airtight container. Cookies can be securely wrapped and frozen up to 2 months.

■ Festive Cookie Bars

Makes 3½ to 4 dozen bars

BOTTOM LAYER
1¼ cups all-purpose flour
1 teaspoon granulated sugar
1 teaspoon baking powder
   Dash salt
⅔ cup butter or margarine
2 tablespoons cold coffee or water
1 egg yolk
1 package (12 ounces) real semisweet
   chocolate pieces

TOP LAYER
½ cup butter or margarine, softened
1 cup granulated sugar
1 tablespoon vanilla
2 eggs plus 1 egg white
1 cup SUN-MAID® Raisins
1 cup DIAMOND® Walnuts
   Powdered sugar, for garnish

To prepare Bottom Layer: In large bowl, combine flour, granulated sugar, baking powder and salt. Cut in butter until mixture resembles coarse crumbs. In small bowl, mix coffee and egg yolk to blend; stir into flour mixture to moisten evenly. Form dough into a roll. With floured fingertips, press evenly onto bottom of greased 15×10-inch jelly-roll pan. (Layer will be thin.) Bake in preheated 350°F oven 10 minutes. Sprinkle chocolate pieces evenly over crust; return to oven 2 minutes to melt chocolate. Remove from oven; spread evenly with spatula. Let stand several minutes to set.

To prepare Top Layer: In large bowl, cream butter, granulated sugar and vanilla. Beat in eggs and egg white, one at a time, mixing well after each addition. (Mixture will appear slightly curdled.) Stir in raisins and walnuts. Spread evenly over chocolate layer. Return to oven; bake 20 to 25 minutes or until top is browned. Dust with powdered sugar. Cool in pan; cut into bars.

Note: Cookies freeze well.

Hershey's Great American Chocolate Chip Cookies

■ Hershey's Great American Chocolate Chip Cookies

About 6 dozen cookies

  1 cup butter, softened
  ¾ cup granulated sugar
  ¾ cup packed light brown sugar
  1 teaspoon vanilla extract
  2 eggs
2¼ cups all-purpose flour
  1 teaspoon baking soda
  ½ teaspoon salt
  2 cups (12-ounce package) HERSHEY'S Semi-Sweet Chocolate Chips
  1 cup chopped nuts (optional)

Cream butter, granulated sugar, brown sugar and vanilla in large mixer bowl until light and fluffy. Add eggs; beat well. Combine flour, baking soda and salt; gradually add to creamed mixture. Beat well. Stir in chocolate chips and nuts.

Drop by teaspoonfuls onto ungreased cookie sheet. Bake at 375° for 8 to 10 minutes or until lightly browned. Cool slightly. Remove from cookie sheet; cool completely on wire rack.

VARIATION
Milk Chocolate Chip Cookies: Substitute 2 cups (11.5-ounce package) HERSHEY'S Milk Chocolate Chips for the semi-sweet chocolate chips.

■ Chocolate Brittle Drops

Makes 2 dozen

  4 squares BAKER'S® Semi-Sweet Chocolate
1½ cups (½ lb.) coarsely crushed peanut brittle

Melt chocolate in saucepan over very low heat, stirring constantly. Remove from heat and stir in peanut brittle. Drop from teaspoon onto waxed paper. Let stand until chocolate is firm.

■ Peanut Butter Rice Snacks

Makes about 16 squares

  1 cup light corn syrup
  ½ cup granulated sugar
  ½ cup packed brown sugar
  1 cup crunchy peanut butter
  6 cups RICE CHEX® Brand Cereal

Line 9×9-inch pan with waxed paper. Combine corn syrup and sugars in large saucepan. Cook over medium heat just until mixture comes to a boil, stirring frequently. Remove from heat. Stir in peanut butter until well combined. Gradually add cereal, stirring until all pieces are evenly coated. Turn into prepared pan. Refrigerate 15 minutes or until firm. Cut into squares. Store covered.

Peanut Butter Rice Snacks

■ Magic Cookie Bars

Makes 24 to 36 bars

½ **cup margarine or butter**
1½ **cups graham cracker *or* other crumbs**
  1 **(14-ounce) can EAGLE® Brand Sweetened**
    Condensed Milk (NOT evaporated milk)
  1 **cup semi-sweet chocolate chips**
  1 **(3½-ounce) can flaked coconut (1⅓ cups)**
  1 **cup chopped nuts**

Preheat oven to 350° (325° for glass dish). In 13×9-inch baking pan, melt margarine in oven. Sprinkle crumbs over margarine; pour sweetened condensed milk evenly over crumbs. Top with remaining ingredients; press down firmly. Bake 25 to 30 minutes or until lightly browned. Cool. Chill if desired. Cut into bars. Store loosely covered at room temperature.

Seven Layer Magic Cookie Bars: Add 1 (6-ounce) package butterscotch flavored chips after chocolate chips.

Double Chocolate Magic Cookie Bars: Increase chocolate chips to 1 (12-ounce) package.

Rainbow Magic Cookie Bars: Add 1 cup plain candy-coated chocolate pieces after chocolate chips.

Magic Peanut Cookie Bars: Omit chocolate chips. Add 2 cups (about ¾ pound) chocolate-covered peanuts.

Mint: Combine ½ teaspoon peppermint extract and 4 drops green food coloring if desired with sweetened condensed milk. Proceed as above.

Mocha: Add 1 tablespoon instant coffee and 1 tablespoon chocolate-flavored syrup with sweetened condensed milk. Proceed as above.

Peanut Butter: Beat ⅓ cup peanut butter with sweetened condensed milk. Proceed as above.

Maple: Combine ½ to 1 teaspoon maple flavoring with sweetened condensed milk. Proceed as above.

Magic Cookie Bars

■ Spiced Apple-Raisin Cookies

Makes about 5 dozen cookies

¾ **cup butter, softened**
  1 **cup packed brown sugar**
  1 **egg**
  1 **teaspoon vanilla**
1½ **cups all-purpose flour**
  1 **teaspoon baking powder**
  ½ **teaspoon baking soda**
  ½ **teaspoon salt**
  ½ **teaspoon ground cinnamon**
  ½ **teaspoon ground nutmeg**
1½ **cups quick-cooking oats, uncooked**
  1 **cup finely chopped unpeeled apple**
  ½ **cup raisins**
  ½ **cup chopped nuts**

In large bowl, cream butter. Gradually add sugar; beat until light and fluffy. Beat in egg and vanilla. In small bowl, combine flour, baking powder, baking soda, salt and spices. Gradually add flour mixture to creamed mixture; blend well. Stir in oats, apple, raisins and nuts. Drop dough by rounded teaspoonfuls 2 inches apart onto lightly greased cookie sheets. Bake in preheated 350° oven 10 to 12 minutes or until lightly browned. Remove to wire racks to cool completely.

Favorite Recipe from **American Dairy Association**

■ Old-Fashioned Molasses Cookies

Makes about 3 dozen cookies

4 cups sifted all-purpose flour
2 teaspoons ARM & HAMMER® Pure Baking Soda
1½ teaspoons ground ginger
½ teaspoon ground cinnamon
⅛ teaspoon salt
1½ cups molasses
½ cup shortening, melted
¼ cup butter or margarine, melted
⅓ cup boiling water
Sugar

In medium bowl, combine flour, baking soda, spices and salt. In large bowl, mix molasses, shortening, butter and water. Add dry ingredients to molasses mixture; blend well. Cover; refrigerate until firm, about 2 hours. Roll out dough ¼ inch thick on well-floured surface. Cut out with 3½-inch cookie cutters; sprinkle with sugar. Place 2 inches apart on ungreased cookie sheets. Bake in preheated 375° oven about 12 minutes. Remove to wire racks to cool.

■ Oatmeal Macaroons

Makes 4½ dozen cookies

1¼ cups all-purpose flour
1 teaspoon baking soda
1 cup margarine, softened
1 cup packed brown sugar
2 eggs
½ teaspoon almond extract
3 cups QUAKER® Oats (quick or old-fashioned, uncooked)
1 package (4 ounces) flaked or shredded coconut

In medium bowl, combine flour and baking soda. In large bowl, cream margarine and sugar until light and fluffy. Blend in eggs and almond extract. Add flour mixture; mix well. Stir in oats and coconut. Drop dough by rounded teaspoonfuls onto greased cookie sheets. Bake in preheated 350° oven 10 minutes or until light golden brown. Let cookies cool 1 minute before removing them from cookie sheets to wire racks.

■ Pinwheels and Checkerboards

Makes about 5 dozen

2 cups flour
1 teaspoon CALUMET® Baking Powder
½ teaspoon salt
⅔ cup butter or margarine
1 cup sugar
1 egg
1 teaspoon vanilla
2 squares BAKER'S® Unsweetened Chocolate, melted

Mix flour, baking powder and salt; set aside. Cream butter. Gradually add sugar and continue beating until light and fluffy. Add egg and vanilla; beat well. Gradually add flour mixture, mixing well after each addition. Divide dough in half; blend chocolate into one half. Use prepared doughs to make Pinwheels or Checkerboards.

Pinwheels: Roll chocolate and vanilla doughs separately between sheets of waxed paper into 12×8-inch rectangles. Remove top sheets of paper and invert vanilla dough onto chocolate dough. Remove remaining papers. Roll up as for jelly roll; then wrap in waxed paper. Chill until firm, at least 3 hours (or freeze 1 hour). Cut into ¼-inch slices and place on baking sheets. Bake at 375° about 10 minutes, or until cookies just begin to brown around edges. Cool on racks.

Checkerboards: Set out small amount of milk. Roll chocolate and vanilla doughs separately on lightly floured board into 9×4½-inch rectangles. Brush chocolate dough lightly with milk and top with vanilla dough. Using a long sharp knife, cut lengthwise into 3 strips, 1½ inches wide. Stack strips, alternating colors and brushing each layer with milk. Cut lengthwise again into 3 strips, ½ inch wide. Invert middle section so that colors are alternated; brush sides with milk. Press strips together lightly to form a rectangle. Wrap in waxed paper. Chill overnight. Cut into ⅛-inch slices, using a very sharp knife. Place on baking sheets. Bake at 375° for about 8 minutes, or just until white portions begin to brown. Cool on racks.

Top: Checkerboards; bottom: Pinwheels

Gifts From the Kitchen

■ Walnut Christmas Balls

Makes about 1½ dozen sandwich cookies

1 cup California walnuts
⅔ cup powdered sugar
1 cup butter or margarine, softened
1 teaspoon vanilla
1¾ cups all-purpose flour
    Chocolate Filling (recipe follows)

In food processor or blender, process walnuts with 2 tablespoons of the sugar until finely ground; set aside. In large bowl, cream butter and remaining sugar. Beat in vanilla. Add flour and ¾ cup of the walnuts; mix until blended. Roll dough into about 3 dozen walnut-size balls. Place 2 inches apart on ungreased cookie sheets. Bake in preheated 350° oven 10 to 12 minutes or until just golden around edges. Remove to wire racks to cool completely. Prepare Chocolate Filling. Place generous teaspoonful of filling on flat side of half the cookies. Top with remaining cookies, flat side down, forming sandwiches. Roll chocolate edges of cookies in remaining ground walnuts.

Chocolate Filling: Chop 3 squares (1 ounce each) semisweet chocolate into small pieces; place in food processor or blender with ½ teaspoon vanilla. In small saucepan, heat 2 tablespoons *each* butter or margarine and whipping cream over medium heat until hot; pour over chocolate. Process until chocolate is melted, turning machine off and scraping sides as needed. With machine running, gradually add 1 cup powdered sugar; process until smooth.

Favorite Recipe from **Walnut Marketing Board**

■ Cherry Fruit Cake

Makes 1 cake

¾ cup flour
½ teaspoon baking powder
½ teaspoon salt
1 (16 oz.) jar Maraschino cherries, whole, drained
8 ounces diced pitted dates
8 ounces glace pineapple
9 ounces pecan halves
3 eggs
1½ ounces rum
¼ cup light corn syrup

Combine flour, baking powder and salt in large mixing bowl; mix well. Add well-drained cherries, dates, pineapple and pecans. Toss together until fruits and nuts are coated with flour mixture. Beat eggs and rum until blended. Pour over coated fruit and mix thoroughly. Grease one 9×5×3-inch loaf pan; line with parchment paper and grease again. Turn cake mixture into pan, pressing with spatula to pack tightly. Bake at 300°F. 1 hour 45 minutes or until wooden pick inserted near center comes out clean. Cool cake in pan 15 minutes. Remove paper from cake; brush with corn syrup while still warm. Cool completely before serving or storing.

Favorite Recipe from **National Cherry Foundation**

Walnut Christmas Balls

■ Creamy White Fudge

Makes about 2¼ pounds

1½ pounds white confectioners' coating*
1 (14-ounce) can EAGLE® Brand Sweetened Condensed Milk (NOT evaporated milk)
⅛ teaspoon salt
¾ to 1 cup chopped nuts
1½ teaspoons vanilla extract

In heavy saucepan, over low heat, melt confectioners' coating with sweetened condensed milk and salt. Remove from heat; stir in nuts and vanilla. Spread evenly into wax paper-lined 8- or 9-inch square pan. Chill 2 hours or until firm. Turn fudge onto cutting board; peel off paper and cut into squares. Store tightly covered at room temperature.

Microwave: In 2-quart glass measure, combine coating, sweetened condensed milk and salt. Microwave on full power (high) 3 to 5 minutes or until coating melts, stirring after 3 minutes. Stir in nuts and vanilla. Proceed as above.

Praline Fudge: Omit vanilla. Add 1 teaspoon maple flavoring and 1 cup chopped pecans. Proceed as above.

Confetti Fudge: Omit nuts. Add 1 cup chopped mixed candied fruit. Proceed as above.

Rum Raisin Fudge: Omit vanilla. Add 1½ teaspoons white vinegar, 1 teaspoon rum flavoring and ¾ cup raisins. Proceed as above.

Cherry Fudge: Omit nuts. Add 1 cup chopped candied cherries.

White confectioners' coating can be purchased in candy specialty stores.

■ Chocolate Pecan Critters

Makes about 5 dozen

1 (11½-ounce) package milk chocolate chips
1 (6-ounce) package semi-sweet chocolate chips
¼ cup margarine or butter
1 (14-ounce) can EAGLE® Brand Sweetened Condensed Milk (NOT evaporated milk)
⅛ teaspoon salt
2 cups coarsely chopped pecans
2 teaspoons vanilla extract
Pecan halves

In heavy saucepan, over medium heat, melt chips and margarine with sweetened condensed milk and salt. Remove from heat; stir in chopped nuts and vanilla. Drop by teaspoonfuls onto wax paper-lined baking sheets. Top with pecan halves. Chill. Store tightly covered.

Microwave: In 2-quart glass measure, microwave chips, margarine, sweetened condensed milk and salt on full power (high) 3 minutes, stirring after 1½ minutes. Stir to melt chips; stir in chopped nuts and vanilla. Proceed as above.

■ Layered Mint Chocolate Candy

Makes about 1¾ pounds

1 (12-ounce) package semi-sweet chocolate chips
1 (14-ounce) can EAGLE® Brand Sweetened Condensed Milk (NOT evaporated milk)
2 teaspoons vanilla extract
6 ounces white confectioners' coating*
1 tablespoon peppermint extract
Few drops green or red food coloring, optional

In heavy saucepan, over low heat, melt chips with *1 cup* sweetened condensed milk. Stir in vanilla. Spread half the mixture into wax paper-lined 8- or 9-inch square pan; chill 10 minutes or until firm. Hold remaining chocolate mixture at room temperature. In heavy saucepan, over low heat, melt confectioners' coating with remaining sweetened condensed milk. Stir in peppermint extract and food coloring if desired. Spread on chilled chocolate layer; chill 10 minutes longer or until firm. Spread reserved chocolate mixture on mint layer. Chill 2 hours or until firm. Turn onto cutting board; peel off paper and cut into squares. Store loosely covered at room temperature.

White confectioners' coating can be purchased in candy specialty stores.

Clockwise from top: Coconut Rum Balls, Chocolate Pecan Critters, Fruit Bon Bons (page 86), Milk Chocolate Bourbon Balls, Buckeyes (page 87), Foolproof Dark Chocolate Fudge (page 86), Peanut Butter Logs (page 86), Layered Mint Chocolate Candy and Cherry Fudge

■ Coconut Rum Balls

Makes about 8 dozen

> 1 (12-ounce) package vanilla wafer cookies, finely crushed (about 3 cups crumbs)
> 1 (3½-ounce) can flaked coconut (1⅓ cups)
> 1 cup finely chopped nuts
> 1 (14-ounce) can EAGLE® Brand Sweetened Condensed Milk (NOT evaporated milk)
> ¼ cup rum
> Additional flaked coconut or confectioners' sugar

In large mixing bowl, combine crumbs, coconut and nuts. Add sweetened condensed milk and rum; mix well. Chill 4 hours. Shape into 1-inch balls. Roll in coconut. Store tightly covered in refrigerator.

Tip: Flavor of these candies improves after 24 hours. They can be made ahead and stored in refrigerator for several weeks.

■ Milk Chocolate Bourbon Balls

Makes about 5½ dozen

> 1 (12-ounce) package vanilla wafer cookies, finely crushed (about 3 cups crumbs)
> 5 tablespoons bourbon or brandy
> 1 (11½-ounce) package milk chocolate chips
> 1 (14-ounce) can EAGLE® Brand Sweetened Condensed Milk (NOT evaporated milk)
> Finely chopped nuts

In medium mixing bowl, combine crumbs and bourbon. In heavy saucepan, over low heat, melt chips. Remove from heat; add sweetened condensed milk. Gradually add crumb mixture; mix well. Let stand at room temperature 30 minutes or chill. Shape into 1-inch balls; roll in nuts. Store tightly covered.

Tip: Flavor of these candies improves after 24 hours. They can be made ahead and stored in freezer. Thaw before serving.

■ Foolproof Dark Chocolate Fudge

Makes about 2 pounds

3 (6-ounce) packages semi-sweet chocolate chips
1 (14-ounce) can EAGLE® Brand Sweetened Condensed Milk (NOT evaporated milk)
Dash salt
½ to 1 cup chopped nuts
1½ teaspoons vanilla extract

In heavy saucepan, over low heat, melt chips with sweetened condensed milk and salt. Remove from heat; stir in nuts and vanilla. Spread evenly into wax paper-lined 8- or 9-inch square pan. Chill 2 hours or until firm. Turn fudge onto cutting board; peel off paper and cut into squares. Store loosely covered at room temperature.

Microwave: In 1-quart glass measure, combine chips with sweetened condensed milk. Microwave on full power (high) 3 minutes. Stir until chips melt and mixture is smooth. Stir in remaining ingredients. Proceed as above.

Creamy Dark Chocolate Fudge: Melt 2 cups CAMPFIRE® Miniature Marshmallows with chips and sweetened condensed milk. Proceed as above.

Milk Chocolate Fudge: Omit 1 (6-ounce) package semi-sweet chocolate chips. Add 1 cup milk chocolate chips. Proceed as above.

Creamy Milk Chocolate Fudge: Omit 1 (6-ounce) package semi-sweet chocolate chips. Add 1 cup milk chocolate chips and 2 cups CAMPFIRE® Miniature Marshmallows. Proceed as above.

Mexican Chocolate Fudge: Reduce vanilla to 1 teaspoon. Add 1 tablespoon instant coffee and 1 teaspoon ground cinnamon to sweetened condensed milk. Proceed as above.

Butterscotch Fudge: Omit chocolate chips and vanilla. In heavy saucepan, melt 2 (12-ounce) packages butterscotch flavored chips with sweetened condensed milk. Remove from heat; stir in 2 tablespoons white vinegar, ⅛ teaspoon salt, ½ teaspoon maple flavoring and 1 cup chopped nuts. Proceed as above.

■ Peanut Butter Logs

Makes two 12-inch logs

1 (12-ounce) package peanut butter flavored chips
1 (14-ounce) can EAGLE® Brand Sweetened Condensed Milk (NOT evaporated milk)
1 cup CAMPFIRE® Miniature Marshmallows
1 cup chopped peanuts

In heavy saucepan, over low heat, melt chips with sweetened condensed milk. Add marshmallows; stir until melted. Remove from heat; cool 20 minutes. Divide in half; place each portion on a 20-inch piece of wax paper. Shape each into 12-inch log. Roll in nuts. Wrap tightly; chill 2 hours or until firm. Remove paper; cut into ¼-inch slices.

Microwave: In 2-quart glass measure, microwave chips, sweetened condensed milk and marshmallows on full power (high) 4 minutes or until melted, stirring after 2 minutes. Let stand at room temperature 1 hour. Proceed as above.

Peanut Butter Fudge: Stir peanuts into mixture. Spread into wax paper-lined 8- or 9-inch square pan. Chill 2 hours or until firm. Turn fudge onto cutting board; peel off paper and cut into squares.

■ Fruit Bon Bons

Makes about 5 dozen

1 (14-ounce) can EAGLE® Brand Sweetened Condensed Milk (NOT evaporated milk)
2 (7-ounce) packages flaked coconut (5⅓ cups)
1 (6-ounce) package fruit flavor gelatin, any flavor
1 cup ground blanched almonds
1 teaspoon almond extract
Food coloring, optional

In large mixing bowl, combine sweetened condensed milk, coconut, ⅓ *cup* gelatin, almonds, extract and enough food coloring to tint mixture desired shade. Chill 1 hour or until firm enough to handle. Using about ½ tablespoon mixture for each, shape into 1-inch balls. Sprinkle remaining gelatin onto wax paper; roll each ball in gelatin to coat. Place on wax paper-lined baking sheets; chill. Store covered at room temperature or in refrigerator.

■ Buckeyes

Makes about 7 dozen

> 2 (3-ounce) packages cream cheese, softened
> 1 (14-ounce) can EAGLE® Brand Sweetened Condensed Milk (NOT evaporated milk)
> 2 (12-ounce) packages peanut butter flavored chips
> 1 cup finely chopped peanuts
> ½ pound chocolate confectioners' coating*

In large mixer bowl, beat cheese until fluffy. Gradually beat in sweetened condensed milk until smooth. In heavy saucepan, over low heat, melt peanut butter chips; stir into cheese mixture. Add nuts. Chill 2 to 3 hours; shape into 1-inch balls. In small heavy saucepan, over low heat, melt confectioners' coating. With wooden pick, dip each peanut ball into melted coating, not covering completely. Place on wax paper-lined baking sheets until firm. Store covered at room temperature or in refrigerator.

Chocolate confectioners' coating can be purchased in candy specialty stores.

■ Pumpkin Nut Bread

Makes two 9×5-inch loaves

> 3½ cups unsifted flour
> 2 teaspoons baking soda
> 1½ teaspoons ground cinnamon
> ½ teaspoon baking powder
> 2 cups sugar
> ⅔ cup shortening
> 4 eggs
> 1 (16-ounce) can pumpkin (about 2 cups)
> ½ cup water
> 1 (9-ounce) package NONE SUCH® Condensed Mincemeat, crumbled
> 1 cup chopped nuts

Preheat oven to 350°. Stir together flour, baking soda, cinnamon and baking powder; set aside. In large mixer bowl, beat sugar and shortening until fluffy. Add eggs, pumpkin and water; mix well. Stir in flour mixture, mincemeat and nuts. Turn into 2 greased 9×5-inch loaf pans. Bake 55 to 60 minutes or until wooden pick inserted near center comes out clean. Cool 10 minutes; remove from pan. Cool completely.

■ Glazed Popcorn

Makes 2 quarts

> 8 cups popped popcorn
> ¼ cup butter or margarine
> 3 tablespoons light corn syrup
> ½ cup packed light brown sugar or granulated sugar
> 1 package (4-serving size) JELL-O® Brand Gelatin, any flavor

Place popcorn in large bowl. Heat butter and syrup in small saucepan over low heat. Stir in brown sugar and gelatin; bring to a boil over medium heat. Reduce heat to low and gently simmer for 5 minutes. Pour syrup immediately over popcorn, tossing to coat well. Spread popcorn on aluminum-foil-lined 15×10×1-inch pan, using two forks to spread evenly. Bake in preheated 300° oven for 10 minutes. Cool. Remove from pan and break into small pieces.

Rainbow Popcorn: Prepare Glazed Popcorn 3 times, using 3 different gelatin colors, such as strawberry, lemon and lime. Bake as directed and break into pieces. Layer 3 cups of each variety in 3-quart bowl. Serve remaining popcorn at another time. Makes 6 quarts.

Glazed Popcorn

■ Golden Carrot Cake

Makes one 10-inch cake

1 (9-ounce) package NONE SUCH®
   Condensed Mincemeat, crumbled
2 cups finely shredded carrots
½ cup chopped nuts
2 teaspoons grated orange rind
2 cups unsifted flour
1 cup firmly packed light brown sugar
¾ cup vegetable oil
4 eggs
2 teaspoons baking powder
1 teaspoon baking soda
1 teaspoon salt
   Orange Glaze (recipe follows)

Preheat oven to 325°. In large bowl, combine mincemeat, carrots, nuts and rind; toss with ½ *cup* flour and set aside. In large mixer bowl, combine sugar and oil; mix well. Add eggs, 1 at a time, beating well after each addition. Stir together remaining *1½ cups* flour, baking powder, baking soda and salt; gradually add to batter, beating until smooth. Stir in mincemeat mixture. Turn into well-greased and floured 10-inch Bundt® or tube pan. Bake 50 to 60 minutes or until wooden pick comes out clean. Cool 10 minutes; remove from pan. Cool completely. Drizzle with Orange Glaze.

Orange Glaze: In small saucepan, melt 2 tablespoons margarine with 4 teaspoons orange juice. Stir in 1 cup confectioners' sugar and 1 teaspoon grated orange rind; mix well. Makes about ½ cup.

■ Hot Fudge Sauce

Makes about 2 cups

1 (6-ounce) package semi-sweet chocolate
   chips *or* 4 (1-ounce) squares semi-sweet
   chocolate
2 tablespoons margarine or butter
1 (14-ounce) can EAGLE® Brand Sweetened
   Condensed Milk (NOT evaporated milk)
2 tablespoons water
1 teaspoon vanilla extract

In heavy saucepan, over medium heat, melt chips and margarine with sweetened condensed milk and water. Cook and stir constantly until thickened, about 5 minutes. Add vanilla. Serve warm over ice cream or as a fruit dipping sauce. Refrigerate leftovers.

To Reheat: In small heavy saucepan, combine desired amount of sauce with small amount of water. Over low heat, stir constantly until heated through.

Microwave: *In 1-quart glass measure, combine ingredients. Cook on 100% power (high) 3 to 3½ minutes, stirring after each minute. Proceed as above.

VARIATIONS:
Mocha: Add 1 teaspoon instant coffee. Proceed as above.

Toasted Almond: Omit vanilla extract. Add ½ teaspoon almond extract. When sauce is thickened, stir in ½ cup chopped toasted almonds.

Choco-Mint: Omit vanilla extract. Add ½ to 1 teaspoon peppermint extract. Proceed as above.

Spirited: Add ⅓ cup almond, coffee, mint *or* orange-flavored liqueur after mixture has thickened.

Mexican: Omit water. Add 2 tablespoons coffee-flavored liqueur *or* 1 teaspoon instant coffee dissolved in 2 tablespoons water and 1 teaspoon ground cinnamon after mixture has thickened.

Microwave ovens vary in wattage and power output; cooking times may need to be adjusted.

Golden Carrot Cake

Almond Lemon Pound Cake

■ Almond Lemon Pound Cake

Makes 1 loaf

> 2 cups cake flour
> ½ teaspoon cream of tartar
> ½ teaspoon salt
> 1 cup butter or margarine, softened
> 1 cup granulated sugar
> 4 eggs
> 5 tablespoons lemon juice
> 1¼ cups BLUE DIAMOND® Chopped Natural
>   Almonds, toasted
> ½ cup powdered sugar
> ½ teaspoon vanilla

In small bowl, combine flour, cream of tartar and salt. In large bowl, cream butter and granulated sugar. Add eggs, 1 at a time, beating well after each addition. Beat in 2 tablespoons of the lemon juice. Gradually add flour mixture; mix thoroughly. Fold in 1 cup of the almonds. Pour batter into greased 9×5×3-inch loaf pan. Sprinkle top with remaining ¼ cup almonds. Bake in preheated 325° oven 1 hour or until toothpick inserted into center comes out clean. Meanwhile, in small saucepan, combine powdered sugar, remaining 3 tablespoons lemon juice and the vanilla. Stir over medium heat until sugar is dissolved. Remove cake from oven. Drizzle hot glaze over top. Let cool in pan on wire rack 15 minutes. Loosen edges; remove from pan. Cool completely on wire rack.

Favorite Recipe from **Blue Diamond Growers**

■ Toasted Pecan Toffee Bars

Makes 3 dozen bars

> 2 cups all-purpose flour
> 1 cup packed brown sugar
> 1 cup LAND O LAKES® Sweet Cream Butter,
>   softened
> 1 teaspoon vanilla
> ½ teaspoon ground cinnamon
> 1 cup chopped pecans, toasted
> 1 cup milk chocolate chips

In large bowl, combine flour, sugar, butter, vanilla and cinnamon; beat until crumbly. Stir in ¾ cup of the pecans and ½ cup of the chips. Press into greased 13×9×2-inch pan. Bake in preheated 350° oven 25 to 30 minutes or until edges are lightly browned. Remove from oven. Immediately sprinkle with remaining ½ cup chips; let stand 5 minutes. Slightly swirl chips as they melt; leave some whole for a marbled effect. *Do not spread chips.* Sprinkle with remaining ¼ cup pecans. Cool completely in pan on wire rack. Cut into bars.

■ Chocolate Truffles

Makes about 6 dozen

**3 (6-ounce) packages semi-sweet chocolate
   chips**
**1 (14-ounce) can EAGLE® Brand Sweetened
   Condensed Milk (NOT evaporated milk)**
1 tablespoon vanilla extract
   **Finely chopped nuts, flaked coconut,
   chocolate sprinkles, colored sprinkles,
   unsweetened cocoa *or* colored sugar**

In heavy saucepan, over low heat, melt chips with
sweetened condensed milk. Remove from heat;
stir in vanilla. Chill 2 hours or until firm. Shape
into 1-inch balls; roll in any of the above coatings.
Chill 1 hour or until firm. Store covered at room
temperature.

Microwave: In 1-quart glass measure, combine
chips and sweetened condensed milk. Microwave
on full power (high) 3 minutes, stirring after 1½
minutes. Stir until smooth. Proceed as above.

Amaretto: Omit vanilla. Add 3 tablespoons
amaretto or other almond-flavored liqueur and ½
teaspoon almond extract. Roll in finely chopped
toasted almonds.

Orange: Omit vanilla. Add 3 tablespoons orange-
flavored liqueur. Roll in finely chopped toasted
almonds mixed with finely grated orange rind.

Rum: Omit vanilla. Add ¼ cup dark rum. Roll in
flaked coconut.

Bourbon: Omit vanilla. Add 3 tablespoons
bourbon. Roll in finely chopped toasted nuts.

■ Mint Cream Liqueur

Makes about 1 quart

**1 (14-ounce) can EAGLE® Brand Sweetened
   Condensed Milk (NOT evaporated milk)**
1¼ cups mint-flavored liqueur
**1 cup (½ pint) BORDEN® or MEADOW GOLD®
   Whipping *or* Coffee Cream**

In blender container, combine ingredients; blend
until smooth. Serve over ice if desired. Store
tightly covered in refrigerator. Stir before serving.
Refrigerate leftovers.

Chocolate Truffles

■ Chewy Chocolate Candies

Makes 2 dozen

½ pound soft caramels
2 tablespoons heavy cream
1 cup (about) pecan halves
4 squares BAKER'S® Semi-Sweet Chocolate,
   melted and cooled

Heat caramels with cream in saucepan over very low heat, stirring constantly. Cool 10 minutes. Set pecans on lightly buttered baking sheets in clusters of 3. Spoon caramel mixture over nuts, leaving outer ends of nuts showing. Let stand to set, about 30 minutes. Spread melted chocolate over caramel mixture.

■ Cherry Pecan Pound Cake

Makes 1 loaf

1 cup butter or margarine, softened
1 cup sugar
4 eggs
1 teaspoon vanilla
½ teaspoon almond extract
½ teaspoon salt
⅛ teaspoon ground nutmeg or mace
1½ cups all-purpose flour
1 jar (6 ounces) maraschino cherries,
   drained and chopped
¼ cup chopped pecans

In large bowl, beat butter and sugar until light and fluffy. Add eggs, vanilla, almond extract, salt and nutmeg; beat until thoroughly blended. Stir in flour, ½ cup at a time, mixing just until blended. Stir in cherries and pecans. Spread batter evenly in greased and floured 9×5×3-inch loaf pan. Bake in preheated 325°oven 60 to 70 minutes or until toothpick inserted near center comes out clean. Let cool in pan on wire rack 10 minutes. Loosen edges; remove from pan. Cool completely on wire rack.

Favorite Recipe from **American Egg Board**

■ Hot Cocoa Mix

Makes about 3 cups

1 cup CREMORA® Non-Dairy Creamer*
1 cup nonfat dry milk
¼ to 1 cup sugar
½ cup unsweetened cocoa

In medium bowl, combine ingredients; mix well. Store in airtight container. To serve, spoon 3 heaping tablespoons mix into mug; add ¾ cup boiling water. Stir.

Mocha: Add ¼ cup instant coffee.

Mexican: Add 1 teaspoon ground cinnamon.

Low-calorie: Omit sugar. Add 15 envelopes low-calorie sweetener with NutraSweet® *or* 2 teaspoons (5 envelopes) low-calorie granulated sugar substitute. To serve, spoon 2 heaping tablespoons into mug; add ¾ cup boiling water. Stir.

Cremora is a coffee whitener and should not be used as a milk replacement.

■ Pineapple-Almond Cheese Spread

Makes 4 cups

2 cans (8 ounces each) DOLE® Crushed
   Pineapple
1 package (8 ounces) cream cheese, softened
4 cups shredded sharp Cheddar cheese
½ cup mayonnaise
1 tablespoon soy sauce
1 cup DOLE® Chopped Natural Almonds,
   toasted
½ cup finely chopped DOLE® Green Bell
   Pepper
¼ cup minced green onion or chives
   DOLE® Celery stalks or assorted breads

Drain pineapple. In large bowl, beat cream cheese until smooth; beat in Cheddar cheese, mayonnaise and soy sauce until smooth. Stir in pineapple, almonds, green pepper and onion. Refrigerate, covered. Use to stuff celery stalks or serve as dip with assorted breads. Serve at room temperature.

Homemade Cream Liqueurs

■ Homemade Cream Liqueurs

Makes about 1 quart

> 1 (14-ounce) can EAGLE® Brand Sweetened
>   Condensed Milk (NOT evaporated milk)
> 1¼ cups flavored liqueur (almond, coffee,
>   orange *or* mint)
> 1 cup (½ pint) BORDEN® or MEADOW GOLD®
>   Whipping or Coffee Cream

In blender container, combine all ingredients;
blend until smooth. Serve over ice and garnish if
desired. Store tightly covered in refrigerator. Stir
before serving.

■ Peppered Pecans

Makes 3 cups

> 3 tablespoons butter or margarine
> 3 cloves garlic, minced
> 1½ teaspoons TABASCO® pepper sauce
> ½ teaspoon salt
> 3 cups pecan halves

Preheat oven to 250°F. In small skillet melt butter.
Add garlic, Tabasco® sauce and salt; cook 1
minute. Toss pecans with butter mixture; spread
in single layer on baking sheet. Bake 1 hour or
until pecans are crisp; stir occasionally.

■ Classic Fudge

Makes 1 pound or about 1½ dozen pieces

> 2 squares BAKER'S® Unsweetened Chocolate
> ¾ cup milk
> 2 cups sugar
>   Dash of salt
> 2 tablespoons butter or margarine
> 1 teaspoon vanilla

Place chocolate and milk in heavy saucepan. Stir
constantly over very low heat until smooth and
slightly thickened, about 5 minutes. Add sugar
and salt; stir over medium heat until sugar is
dissolved and mixture boils. Continue boiling,
without stirring, until small amount of mixture
forms a soft ball in cold water (or to a temperature
of 234°).

Remove from heat; add butter and vanilla. *Do not
stir.* Cool to lukewarm (110°). Beat until mixture
begins to lose its gloss and holds its shape. Pour at
once into buttered 8×4-inch loaf pan. Cool until
set; then cut into squares. Let stand in pan until
firm.

Acknowledgments

The publishers would like to thank the companies and organizations listed below for the use of their recipes in this book.

Almond Board of California
American Dairy Association
American Egg Board
Best Foods, a Division of CPC International Inc.
Blue Diamond Growers
Borden Kitchens, Borden, Inc.
Campbell Soup Company
Carnation Evaporated Milk
Checkerboard Kitchens, Ralston Purina Company
Church & Dwight Co., Inc.
Cribari & Sons Winery
The Dole Food Company
Durkee-French Foods, Division of Reckitt Colman Inc.
Florida Department of Citrus
General Foods Corporation
Hershey Foods Corporation
Keebler Company
Kraft, Inc.
Land O' Lakes, Inc.

Libby's Pumpkin, Division of Carnation Company
Maidstone Wine & Spirits, Inc.
McIlhenny Company
National Cherry Foundation
National Live Stock and Meat Board
National Pecan Marketing Council, Inc.
National Pork Producers Council
National Turkey Federation
Norseland Foods, Inc.
Oklahoma Peanut Commission
Pet Incorporated
Procter & Gamble
The Quaker Oats Company
Sun-Diamond Growers of California
Swift-Eckrich, Inc.
Thomas J. Lipton, Inc.
Walnut Marketing Board
Washington Apple Commission
Western New York Apple Growers Association, Inc.
Wisconsin Milk Marketing Board

Photo Credits

The publishers would like to thank the companies and organizations listed below for the use of their photographs in this book.

American Dairy Association
Best Foods, a Division of CPC International Inc.
Blue Diamond Growers
Borden Kitchens, Borden, Inc.
Campbell Soup Company
Checkerboard Kitchens, Ralston Purina Company
The Dole Food Company
Durkee-French Foods, Division of Reckitt Colman Inc.
General Foods Corporation
Hershey Foods Corporation
Keebler Company

Kraft, Inc.
Land O' Lakes, Inc.
National Pecan Marketing Council, Inc.
National Pork Producers Council
National Turkey Federation
Pet Incorporated
Procter & Gamble
Sun-Diamond Growers of California
Swift-Eckrich, Inc.
Thomas J. Lipton, Inc.
Walnut Marketing Board
Wisconsin Milk Marketing Board